A MAN RAISED UP

Recollections and Reflections

on

Venerable Edmund Rice

presented in 1994
on the occasion of the
150th Anniversary of his death.

ELO PUBLICATIONS
IN ASSOCIATION WITH THE
CONGREGATION OF CHRISTIAN BROTHERS
MARCH 1994

First published in March 1994
by Elo Publications, Reuben Avenue, Dublin 8, Ireland
in association with the
Congregation of Christian Brothers

ISBN: 0 9519593 7 9

Book design by Patrick Funge
Media Conversion from disk, styling and
outputting by Diskon Technical Services Limited,
48 Reuben Avenue, Dublin 8, Ireland.
Cover design by Bill Bolger, MSDI, MICAD
Printed and bound by Elo Press Limited,
Dublin 8, Ireland.

Contents

Contributors

DESMOND RUSHE is the well-known journalist who for many years wrote Tatler's Parade in the *Irish Independent* newspaper. He is the author of the most recent biography of Edmund Rice, *Edmund Rice: The Man and His Times* (1981).

ASSUMPTA O'NEILL is a Presentation Sister and teaches in Waterford. She is a graduate of UCC with an MA in History. She has long been interested in the story of Edmund Rice and the early sisters of the Presentation in Waterford.

MICHAEL AUSTIN CONNOLLY, Christian Brother, is Procurator-General of the Congregation of Christian Brothers since 1978. He is resident in Rome. He is a graduate of NUI with the degree of MA in Ancient Classics and HDipEd. He is also a Doctor-in-Letters from the Catholic University of Milan.

J. MATTHEW FEHENEY is a member of the Presentation Brothers. He is a keen genealogist and has published several articles and a book on family history, *The Ranahans of Iverus* (1987). He is Director of the Christian Formation Resource Centre in Cork.

FRANK KEANE, Christian Brother, is a graduate of NUI and Marino Institute of Education. He was awarded a Postgraduate Diploma in Religious Formation by the Metropolitan College, St. Louis University, St. Louis, USA. He is a regular contributor to newspapers, magazines and radio on Edmund Rice. At present he is Curator of the Blessed Sacrament Chapel and Edmund Rice Centre, Mount Sion, Waterford.

DANIEL V. KELLEHER, Christian Brother, is a graduate of the University of London and of Boston College where he was awarded Master's degrees. He also holds a PhD from the National University of Ireland. Published work: *James Dominic Burke, a Pioneer of Irish Education* (Irish Academic Press 1988); he is at present preparing for publication a book entitled *The Maynooth Decrees!* He is a member of the staff of Ard Scoil Rís, Limerick.

LIAM P. Ó CAITHNIA, Christian Brother, holds Masters and Doctors degrees from NUI. Published work: *Scéal na hIománá*, *Apalóga na bhFilí*, *Micheál Cíosóg*, *Báirí Cos in Éirinn* and, with Tomás Ó Fiaich, *Art Mac Bionaid: Dánta*. At present he is engaged in prising open troublesome problems in the life of Venerable Edmund Rice and bringing to a conclusion a detailed study of Penal Faith in Ireland, 1600-1800 AD. He lives in the Brothers' community, North Richmond Street, Dublin.

SEÁN Ó CEARBHAILL, Christian Brother, holds master's degrees in History and Spirituality. He is the author of many articles in Irish and English. He has published three volumes of Irish poetry. He has had a life-long interest in Edmund Rice and resides in Mount Sion, Waterford.

7

Acknowledgments

I wish to thank the following for permission to use illustrations and photographs in this volume:

Br. Dominic Sassi, Provincial Superior, St. Mary's Province, England, and Br. J. T. Dunne for photographs from Edmund Ignatius Rice, A Spiritual Profile, A. L. O'Toole, Burleigh Press, Bristol, 1985.

Br. Columba Normoyle for illustrations from A Tree is Planted, (Private Publication), 1975 and Memories of Edmund Rice, (Private Publication),1985.

Mr. Desmond Kyne for scenes from the icon of Edmund Rice.

Foreword

M ANY EVENTS are being promoted in 1994 to mark the occasion of the 150th Anniversary of the death of Edmund Rice, Founder of the Congregations of the Presentation and Christian Brothers. This volume of recollections and reflections is just one approach to honour the memory of a great man to whom the Brothers in the Congregations he founded, and indeed so many others, owe their inspiration.

This collection owes much in its turn to the great tradition of research and scholarship that has been built up over the years around the study of Edmund Rice, his life and times. Hence, mention is made in the notes and source material appended to these essays of the work of Desmond Rushe, Brothers Columba Normoyle, Leonard O'Toole, William Gillespie, David Fitzpatrick, Mark Hill, Dominic Burke, and going right back to the earliest Christian Brother source, Origin, more than likely the work of one of Edmund Rice's earliest companions, Br. E. A. Dunphy. If reading and reflecting on the essays offered here should inspire others to delve more deeply and prayerfully into the study of the legacy of Edmund Rice then the effort involved in putting the collection together will have been well rewarded. To paraphrase Br. Seán Ó Cearbhaill (A Memory that Lived and a Charity that Died): 'They give us a taste for more and urge us to dig deeper and to search further'.

I think it important to stress that these essays set out to offer but a taste, a flavour, a glimpse of Edmund. So much more could be written, so many aspects of his life and spirituality not touched upon here could be, and indeed deserve to be, highlighted, but await another day and other pens.

The writers were free to choose their own topic. Consequently there is no discernible theme save that of Edmund Rice himself. It did, however, seem appropriate to me to begin with the biographical sketch, The Man from Callan, and to end with The Death of Brother Edmund Ignatius Rice in the Words of an Eyewitness. In between are studies of aspects of Edmund's spirituality, his family and social background, the death of his wife, his Dublin foundations, and the struggle to overcome opposition to his schools. The essay on Edmund Rice's involvement with

A Man Raised Up

the setting up of the Presentation Sisters school in Waterford is indicative of the Christian Brother links with the Presentation Congregations of Brothers and Sisters, a link that is being given greater tangible expression in more recent times.

In thanking all those good people who have helped to put this book together I wish to pay special tribute to the contributors. They are all busy people and yet lavished time unstintingly on preparing the scripts and being open to amending them. All of them looked on their part in the project as a labour of love. Their regard, even devotion, for Edmund Rice is everywhere evident, not least in the easy familiarity which they frequently refer to him as 'the Founder'. All will be rewarded if this little book should help in bringing Edmund Rice into the hearts and homes of the growing number of people, out and beyond his Brothers and Sisters, who are finding inspiration from his example.

My thanks also to the staff of the Edmund Rice Anniversary Office in Dublin – Sheila Deegan, Robert Stocker, Thomas Moore, Mike Deegan and Br. Tom Connolly – all busy people, too, but who played a not insignificant role in preparing this book for publication. Also Br. Clem McCullough, Mr. Dave Magennis and Br. Dermot O'Neill for proof reading assistance, and the staff of Elo Press for their professionalism, kindness and courtesy.

Br. P. S. Carroll
Feast of St. Joseph
March 1994

Introduction

WERE A MODERN equivalent of Edmund Rice to behave as Edmund behaved almost two centuries ago, public and media reaction would probably label him as, at best, an eccentric or, at worst, a lunatic. Were one of our present, and numerous, crop of millionaire entrepreneurs to sell not alone his business but also his luxurious home, and to devote both himself and the proceeds to a deprived section of the population, his sanity would be questioned. The sacrifice of wealth, comfort and social status in the interests of the severely marginalised is not something which conforms to prevailing attitudes of a world obsessed with self and material possessions.

Edmund Rice enjoyed wealth, comfort and social status. His business in Waterford was thriving and expanding: it provisioned the ships (as many as a thousand a year) which called at one of Europe's busiest ports; it supplied the military stationed at Southern Hill; it was a prosperous retail outlet. Pork, beef, butter, salt, hay and straw were among the commodities with which it dealt in bulk, and the animals which it slaughtered, dressed, salted and packed came from Carlow, Kilkenny, Tipperary, the midland counties and as far away as Limerick. For business acumen, Edmund could take his place with any of today's successful entrepreneurs: he was a Feargal Quinn or a Ben Dunne of his time and, in terms of current money values, he would have belonged to the millionaire category.

Then, in his thirties and with more commercial heights to scale and riches to accumulate, he sold his business and his comfortable home in Arundel Place. His new centre of operation became a stable which he had converted into classrooms (horse stables were numerous and commodious at the time), and his new place of abode became the loft above the stable. Some of his business friends considered him foolish and impractical: the terms would be more harsh and abrasive now, for the Christian vision which motivated him, the faith which sustained him and the prayer which nourished him are much less comprehensible to the materialistic, secular and hedonistic society of today. And anyway, it would be argued, the conditions which inspired Edmund to his absurd, or heroic behaviour no longer apply.

11

Which is a monstrous lie. The deprived, marginalised and suffering are there still, in vastly increased numbers throughout the world, and the need for Rice-like gestures is correspondingly greater. The mistake is to relate Edmund Rice to the early 1800s and to Waterford, or Ireland. The truth is that he belongs to all times and to all places – an inspiration and a challenge then, now and over all the years to come.

Desmond Rushe

The Man from Callan

Liam P. Ó Caithnia, CFC

H IS HOLINESS Pope John Paul II in September 1992 beatified
seventeen Irish martyrs who died for the Faith in Ireland
in the sixteenth and seventeenth centuries. The Causes of
Beatification of several other Irish men and women, although
not martyrs, have also been under consideration for some years
past notably those of Catherine Macauley, Foundress of the Irish
Sisters of Mercy, the largest religious order in the Catholic Church,
and Edmund Rice, Founder of the Christian Brothers and of the
Presentation Brothers. Both Causes have passed two of the last
three stages in the process of Beatification and we pray earnestly
whilst awaiting hopefully the judgement of the Holy See in its
assessment of the merits of the miracles submitted to it on behalf
of each of them respectively.

Edmund Rice was born on a farm outside the small town of
Callan, about nine miles from Kilkenny, in 1762, just nine years
before the first crack appeared in the penal laws – the Bogland Act
of 1771 when, it could be argued, one penal law replaced another!
He was the fourth of seven sons and had two step-sisters by the
previous marriage of his mother, Margaret Tierney. Because
Callan (and even the town of Kilkenny) was Irish-speaking at that
time he was undoubtedly called Éamann at home. The Rices were
comfortable by the standards of their day: the house they lived in
is little changed from what it was and, as a place of pilgrimage,
is one of the most attractive of its kind in or out of Ireland.
The Brothers who teach in the school in Callan have a residence
nearby and there is always one of them present to show people
around the old home of the Rices where a great deal of social
history lies before the eyes of any casual visitor. A couple of yards
away from the old homestead is a beautiful church built in recent
years where one may pray at one's ease, and a side-room where
the famous icon, the work of artist Desmond Kyne, dedicated to
the name and sanctity of Edmund Rice, may be studied without
interference.

The Rice boys were taught at home by a young teacher,
Patrick Grace, who was himself preparing for the priesthood,
and Edmund, after a short stay in Kilkenny where he studied

13

commercial subjects, was apprenticed to his uncle who had a business in the meat trade in Waterford. From the day he got behind a counter the tall, sandy-haired youngster from Callan proved himself to be a businessman of rare ability, a man who drove himself hard and had an eye to the smallest detail. He walked through all the counties of Munster and beyond it, covering as many as possible of the four and a half thousand fairs that were held annually in Ireland at that time, buying sheep and cattle and saying the beads as he went. In fact it was on one such trip that God first called him to a closer union with Himself.

Meanwhile, in games of finance or business Edmund Rice was not a man to miss a trick. Within ten years, when he was about twenty-seven, he had become known all over Waterford as a young man of substance. We are reasonably sure of this because otherwise the death of his very young wife (sixteen or seventeen years old?) in 1789 would not have been noted, as it was, in several newspapers of the day – particularly since she was but one of tens of thousands who died of the plague in that year.

Edmund Rice loved his business, loved the world, loved the money, was ambitious for success and had every intention of making it to the top – penal law or no penal law! He had the brain of a shrewd and natural lawyer and all the ramifications of his buying and selling of property will probably never be fully known because, as a Catholic, he had to cover his traces. Much of his wealth derived from the fact that he was a ship's chandler with a steadily increasing trade because of the vessels that passed endlessly through the port of Waterford.

The man from Callan did excellent business and, when he was twenty-three or twenty-four years old he got married but lost his wife within a year or two, as already noted and was left with a baby daughter who never married and who appears to have been delicate all her life. The nature of her delicacy is not known nor is there any clear evidence, indeed any evidence at all, that she was handicapped, physically or mentally, as some writers suggest.

The study of Edmund Rice at this time is one of absorbing interest. Having lost his wife he was now free to follow any one of three or four courses: he could have given all his time and attention to the business he valued so highly or he could have sought another wife, for he had youth, money and social standing on his side. Most of his biographers overlook the fact, acknowledged by Catholic and ascendancy commentators alike, that men like him, who had got rich through dealing with fellow-Catholics and having their support, showed virtually no interest in them or loyalty to them (or to their clergy) and offered them no solace when they could have done so. They ceased to allow their sons to be educated in Catholic colleges on the Continent or to support those colleges and they were no longer satisfied to permit their sons to pursue a priestly vocation: in the plainest English, they became Castle Catholics.

It is to the everlasting credit of Edmund Rice that he did not react to his wealth and prestige in this way. A deeply spiritual man who had come from a country home that was comfortable, if not precisely well-off, he quickly learned the meaning of poverty, vice and ignorance while helping young prostitutes and their sea-going friends in the quays and back-lanes of Waterford. The poor got poorer by the day and were caught in a trap of squalor and want and the vices attendant on them. Seeing this he began to understand two facts that were to become, in time, overwhelming convictions: firstly, that not money or property or any such temporal trinkets could make a people free – nothing but education could do that. Secondly, he became no less convinced that once men and women had been destroyed by vice the battle to raise them up was well-nigh hopeless – short of a miracle of grace. Therefore he seems to have gathered a small circle of boys whom he trained to seek out the weaker ones and to attract them to himself. The truth of this striking fact, as the older Waterford informants recalled it, seems to me to be worthy of very serious consideration.

After 1789 Edmund Rice had to deal with the loneliness that followed the death of his young wife and to make provision for the care of his baby girl. More and more he began to look for consolation and strength to two sources: prayer and sacred scripture. Having come from a devout Catholic family he is believed and remembered to have been religiously inclined all his life but, despite these assurances and some unverified traditions, there is little clear evidence that his religious practice was especially notable. Honesty and integrity had been associated with him at all times but, until the death of his wife, he was seen to be a man intent on extending his business and increasing his wealth. That fact needs to be stressed because the sacrifice he

15

made before he was forty was, for him more than most men, acutely hurtful. What we love most and have worked hardest for is most difficult to part with! Edmund Rice's sacrifice was the decision to go, sell what he had, give to the poor and follow the Man of Galilee. He did that however with a determination equal to what he had previously shown in the pursuit of money. He turned his back on what he had held most precious and fought hardest for – what we would call nowadays his predominant passion – money, wealth – and staked his life on the word of Christ! It is at this juncture in his life that, in my view, many people short-change Edmund Rice. Most of those who are familiar with his odyssey will concede that his *sin* as Pearse might have said, was to have taken Christ at his word! I do not think so: there was significantly more to it than that. We might comprehend, however dimly, the nature and degree of his sacrifice if we could but grasp the extent of the void that had grown through centuries of injustice between what were known as the lower orders and the upper classes. This chasm dared not be crossed without offending the sensibilities of the *better classes* – every last one of them – and to do so openly, even in the name of Christian charity, was to provoke intense and unremitting hostility. To act in this way was to pose as a prophet or to prance like a buffoon. Nobody appreciated that better than Edmund Rice for already he had crossed the thresholds of shanty and lace curtain alike: he had mixed in Waterford with those who had arrived and had sought and suffered with those who would never arrive. He knew the rules!

From now on he became a man apart. Prayer, daily Mass, the frequent reception of the Eucharist, long hours before the Blessed Sacrament, endless charity to the poor and broken creatures who asked his help, constant support of pious and charitable institutions, and prayerful reflection on the Old and New Testaments: little by little these things captured his attention until eventually he had become a changed man.

In 1803 he gave up house and home, business and lifestyle and he chose to do so right there, in Waterford City, where he had lived in increasing prosperity for more than twenty years and where he was now to become an object of curiosity under the inquisitive eyes of former associates. He moved home from the comfort and elegance of Arundel Place to the poverty and misery of Ballybricken: a distance of one million miles! Here he began to engage in that

Westcourt – exterior

Waterford, c.1800

one profession in life for which he was, in the received sense, least qualified and scarcely endowed at all: teaching the poorest of the Penal poor. Despite my deep respect and affection for this man – one of the most remarkable ever to have come from our country – I feel obliged to confess that I think he could scarcely have been less prepared than he was for the desperate task to which he now addressed himself.

We may rest assured that he can have known nothing whatever about normal teaching methods, blackboard behaviour or class-room delinquency nor did he have access to any of the endless aids that are now almost universally available to those who are engaged in helping youthful learners. Did he have chalk or duster? A blackboard? Pencils, pens, ink or copybooks? And if he had any of these primitive aids what did he know about them or about the use of them? With the greatest respect in the world I wonder how good a communicator was he? Even today, more than two hundred years after the death of his wife, we do not know her name, surname, origin, religious belief or family background nor do we know how she died or where. Two of the Brothers who must have known him best were John Austin Grace who lived within a few miles of Callan and Patrick Corbett from Sliabh na mBan. Both knew him well for many years but Br. Grace did not know how many brothers he had and Pat Corbett thought his father's name was Nicholas (it was Robert!) and this at a time in Ireland when *tracing* was a national pastime! Tom Heron of Callan spared no praise on the Rices, a family for whom he harboured the greatest admiration but, he confessed, "there was an aloofness about them all".

Since he lived, not in the town of Callan but in a hamlet outside it, Edmund Rice can have known but very little concerning the control of children who came from drunken homes and whose parents, brutalised and vitiated by poverty, hunger and despair had never known self-respect or the tenderness, support and love of a home and family. No experienced teacher would willingly face such a trauma as this: what hope could a normal young businessman have of surviving it in the town where he had carved out his own elegant niche – and to do so *on his own*? Is it not easy to hear the sagacious ones?: "He must be out of his mind!" In the Pauline sense he may well have been that – a fool for Christ's sake!

The Man from Callan

I have suggested that he was not notably endowed by nature for the task of teaching. I say it because whatever other gift a teacher needs to have, he or she must be a *communicator* and there is very little in the life of this extraordinary man to suggest that he had that enviable gift to any notable degree – if at all? Yet God called him – and he followed – and having made his decision, nothing by the grace of God, could ever make him renege on it! It is quite certain however that apart from a noteworthy faith in Divine Providence he was an excellent administrator, was acutely sensitive to the niceties of the law – at that time still largely a Penal Law – and had such a grasp of financial details as was shared by very few Catholics in the early nineteenth century. Such gifts and such expertise were rare among them because of their long deprivation. Edmund Rice therefore had something special to offer when he brought such gifts to the service of God not only through founding a school (at Mount Sion, Waterford) and drawing up a school programme that was Christian and national in character but attracting men young and not so young to follow him in a religious congregation which he himself set about founding. God in His wisdom knew that teachers and methods would come with time: meanwhile an administrator was required, one that could handle financial, legal and administrative problems with some degree of expertise. With respect He chose his man well!

What moved Edmund Rice to leave his comfortable home in Waterford to sell his thriving business and dedicate himself to the cause of poor boys was a threefold conviction. He was satisfied that the only cause worth serving at the end of the day was the cause of Christ, that we cannot pretend to serve him unless we serve the Christ who is visible to us in every one of our poorest neighbours and that the poorest of all, so far as he could see, were the children who owned nothing, who knew nothing, who could hope for nothing. They were children without hope: they were *hope*-less. Dying like lice in filthy hovels, they were far worse off than today's travellers. Nobody wanted them, nobody cared for them, fed them, taught them, understood them, was ready to sacrifice himself for them. Yet they were all Christ's as Hopkins reminds us "for Christ plays in ten thousand places, lovely . . . to the Father through the features of men's faces."

The Callan-man with the Midas touch heard the call and answered it. We have already alluded to Pearse's perennial

Part of the original Mount Sion

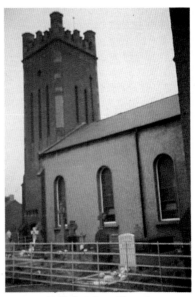

Ballybricken Church

Memorial Chapel and restored Bakehouse

question – one of defiance as well as defence: "Is this my sin before men to have taken Christ at his word?" Not only did Edmund Rice, shrewdest of men, do so but he did it without regret in broad daylight and in the town that he loved so well. And because men of such calibre are rare at any time and acutely so in these times of political strokes, financial finagling and troublesome tribunals, it is our hope and prayer that the Lord through his Church will see fit to beatify him and grant us the assurance we seek: that the way of Edmund Rice was a way to sanctity and that we with all our well-documented faults and human errors may follow him in faith and in hope.

In 1802 he built his first school and religious residence in Waterford at the place now known to all Waterford people as Mount Sion. Slowly – very slowly indeed – young men began to share his vision and joined him in the hope of changing the land. Change it they did: he sent communities to Carrick-on-Suir, Thurles, Dungarvan, Dublin, Britain, Australia and so on. The man who had loved money had learnt equally well to give it away freely and without interest. The man who was not notably voluble in communicating with others seems to have introduced several generations of the poor of Waterford to the knowledge and love of Christ, to a new insight into their own worth and excellence as children of God and consequently to a healthy self-esteem and happy realisation that they were "bought at a great price".

In Mount Sion he had a tailor's shop and a bakery both working full time in the interest of poor boys. He provided them with pious books to bring home and read for their parents both illiterate and non-literate. He held evening classes to prepare adults for Confirmation and also for what were known as 'workers'. 'Workers' were boys who had to leave school at the age of nine to work at menial tasks all over the town if they were to avoid starvation and then returned to the Brothers at any age from 12 to 15 or 16 or even older for classes in religious instruction so that they might be Confirmed. Bit by bit and year by year they persevered in the long hard climb out of their drab huts, cabins and filthy hovels, ghettoes of illiteracy, ignorance, juvenile crime and heartbreaking starvation. Harder even than that was the struggle of the miserably depressed to win back their God-given right to self-respect – an almost impossible task for a people long inured to the insolence injustice and savagery of heartless overlords.

A Man Raised Up

People talk glibly today about the need for continued social mobility partly – and unconsciously perhaps – because they sense the danger that it is slipping away from our society of 'haves' and 'have nots'. Not many of them are aware that social mobility is a peculiarly Christian thing which owes more in this country to the influence of teaching religious orders – *native* ones at that! – than most people ever pause to consider. Even less do they realise that that 'peculiarly Christian thing' as I have called it will survive only so long as people are prepared to fight and make sacrifices for it. One wonders: if social justice – life itself – is to be denied to children even before birth, how long can we hope to see it automatically respected *after* birth? *Ach sin ceist eile*!

Edmund Rice was eighty-two when he died peacefully in Mount Sion, Waterford, in 1844 having suffered much of the heartache, much of the misunderstanding, much of the loneliness that men inhabit who stand aside from our common lot. Most educated Catholics will readily appreciate that the evil one hates a man like Edmund Rice for precisely the reasons for which good people respect him. Satan does not glory in the reign of virtue or of goodness. Edmund Rice therefore had enemies in the Church – even in his own religious brotherhood! – and outside it. He was accused of doing those things precisely that he sought to avoid. He was a man whose hand was endlessly outstretched to bless or to offer a charity or to shake the hand of a fellow Christian. When the Christian Brothers first determined to have his Cause introduced to Rome during 1911-1913 with the blessing of the Irish Hierarchy, one of the Brothers was given the task of collecting whatever memories of him still lingered on in the minds of the people who knew him best especially in Waterford. I find nothing so remarkable in the testimony of these informants (about 250 of them) as the strange uniformity of the opinion, constantly repeated, that he was "a man raised up by God". So universal was this extraordinary conviction that I became concerned that the informants must be answering a trigger question. Television has no monopoly of this well-worn and dishonest ploy! Three things convinced me I was wrong: there was a note of unmistakable integrity echoing through all that these simple unpretentious men and women had to say about the servant of God whom they or their fathers had known and remembered (about twenty of them could remember him personally). Secondly, Br. Mark Hill whose task it was to seek and question, noticed soon enough the frequency of this refrain and wrote to his Superior-General to assure him that he had noticed the phenomenon but that he was *not* triggering a desired answer. Thirdly, if I had any residual doubt it melted away when some informants added casually that this was what *people always said* about Brother Rice: that he was "a man raised up by God." If *vox populi* (the voice of the people) is *vox Dei* (the voice of God) then Edmund Rice was not only beatified but canonised soon after death – if not before it!

The question is frequently asked: Why go to the bother and expense of canonising anyone? Isn't it enough to say that they were holy women and men (more women than men have been formally canonised) than to give them official titles indicating sanctity? (People who pose this question however have no great qualms about acknowledging the titles of Lord X, Lady Y and Viscount Z.) Some concerned people ask whether the money required for the process could not be spent in far more sensible and charitable ways? Above all they say isn't Christ Himself the only intercessor with the Father and why introduce a mere human to intercede for us instead of asking Him to do so? Sometimes these questions are asked with some degree of impatience and veiled hostility but all of them are easily answered for people with unbiased minds. The following are some of the responses that occur to me – though I have omitted some that concern his religious Brothers only:

1. All saints are a *challenge* to us: they set standards and not only for fellow-religious but for all who are prepared to learn. Businessmen, parents – especially those of children who are physically or mentally ill or handicapped – teachers (of course) administrators, people in positions of authority and trust and so on, all have something to learn about Christian living from men like Edmund Rice.

2. They *encourage* us even while challenging us. Edmund Rice suffered a deeper personal tragedy than most, had no professional (teacher) training, had endless financial, administrative and legal headaches. Like all saintly people he is a lesson to us in his profound trust in Divine Providence. Few men or women reflect this confidence as he did – and he referred to it endlessly always using the expression 'Divine Providence'.

3. Many theologians argue in favour of canonisation so that Christ may be made visible in our time. They suggest that the

Holy Spirit inspires the Church to canonise people of exceptional holiness so that despite our weakness and our sinfulness we may be attracted in all ages to and by the phenomenon of sanctity.

4. In gifting a person like Edmund Rice by our prayerful and generous efforts we will as usual be gifted in return. The effort, moreover, will help us to think, pray, remember our best ideals and the apostolate that God has entrusted to us whatever it may be.

5. Finally, we must confess that even in our day there are Catholics who doubt the propriety if not the orthodoxy of praying for gifts and graces through the intercession of *any mere creatures*, howsoever holy – and that includes the intercession of Mary herself, the Blessed Mother of God! Yet St Thomas Aquinas expressly states that the saints who reign together with Christ offer up their prayers to God for men. It is good and useful suppliantly to invoke them and to have recourse to their prayers . . .

Encouraged by this we pray to the holy angels and to men and women, not so that God may learn our petition through them but that by *their* prayers and *their* merits our prayers may be efficacious. I will not quote the Council of Trent (Sess. XXV) on the matter but it is clear and explicit in its assurance that it is good "to invoke the saints and to have recourse to their prayers".

We who are members of the Church of Christ should be fearless and uncompromising in asserting this doctrine that it is a good and salutary thing to pray for the intercession of all those who have died in the friendship of God and Edmund Rice is assuredly one of these. His mortal remains lie in a sarcophagus in the specially-built Edmund Rice Chapel in Mount Sion, Waterford.

Edmund Rice and His Social Milieu

Liam P. Ó Caithnia, CFC

A MONG THE CHARACTERISTICS of the Irish people in the period of Classical Irish poetry, c.1200-1650 A.D., few were as noteworthy or as deplorable as the class distinction ingrained in the society of the time – and for long before it – which divided the haves from the have-nots, the wealthy and the powerful from the poor and the disadvantaged. This is amply apparent in much of the published Classical verse of that period as well as in the major satires: *Comhairle Mhic Clamha*[1], *Commissarius na Cléire*[2] and *Pairlement Chloinne Tomáis*[3] and in other compositions such as *Párliament na mBan*[4], or *The Life and Death of the Most Rev. Francis Kirwan, Bishop of Killala*[5], in the introduction to which Very Rev. Gregory Joyce's connection by blood with "all the best people (in Galway)"[6] was loudly trumpeted. It is obvious moreover in the *relationes status* of the period – in fact virtually every letter of St. Oliver Plunkett bears witness to his deep-rooted conviction of the superiority of those clergymen of whom the great and saintly archbishop could say, in recommending them for a vacant see, that they were members of what in modern times would be called well-heeled families. The fact that they were also pious men and well-educated was not unhelpful. O'Sullivan Béarra noted in 1617:

> that priests of noble parentage, such as had heretofore come from (the seminary in) Santiago did *treble* as much good as the sons of merchants and plebians such as were admitted there in 1617[7].

This was not altogether matter for surprise: it was a common assumption, after all, that the "milesian habits" of laziness and drunkenness were met with exclusively amongst the "lower orders,"[8] in other words, among the poor. The reader will note, in passing – and for further comment – the association of 'merchants' with 'plebians': it was not accidental.

That this form of unchristian class-distinction was still alive and well down even to the eighteenth century is quite apparent in, for example, James Coombes's timely and welcome biography of Bishop (and poet) Seán Ó Briain of Cloyne (1701-1769)[9] the *nobility* of whose immediate ancestry, as well as his absolute

25

dissociation from any unseemly manual work or trade, indicated, it would appear, his suitability for the See of Cloyne[10]! Meanwhile the plain people of God were every bit as opposed as their betters to manual work or trading of any kind though they rarely claimed kinship with the princes of the land. Very occasionally an intelligent clergyman appealed to the people to have sense and to apprentice their sons to a trade. Conchúr Mac Cairteáin, for example, (c.1658-1737), Parish Priest of Glanmire, Co. Cork, besought his people to impart a trade to their offspring:

When they can read and write, give them a trade for life. It is nothing to be ashamed of, even in the best of men, that a person be a tailor, a fuller or a weaver, or to have some other trade. However, it is shameful for him to be a rogue or a pauper, or a scoundrel. Nothing so impoverishes the Irish and makes beggars of them as the lack of a permanent trade. In other nations people do not scorn to teach a life's trade to their offspring, such as that of weaver, bootmaker or smith, since they know that, however hard things may get, they will, as long as they are healthy, make a living through their trade. Be that as it may, we Irish were, until recently, so misfortunate, stupidly proud and nonsensical that the son of a farmer or a nobody, to say nothing of a man of standing or substance, would put his offspring to dealing or to some one of the aforementioned trades.[11]

Even if the Bogland Act of 1771 heralded the advent of a new deal for the downtrodden Catholics, one knows only too well that long-established attitudes die slowly and never merely at the behest of a royal command. The deep disregard for the poor and for manual work was never quite overcome despite the compelling insistence of the New Testament and the example of Nano Nagle, Catherine McAuley, Edmund Rice and the founders of religious institutes which followed later. There was therefore a chasm between the well-off and those who were not so blest, and who counted for nothing and were rarely listened to. There is no lack whatever of evidence in proof of this assertion. Just a year after the passing of the Bogland Act, one James Stewart, M.P. for Tyrone, writing to Charlemont, 23 July 1772, observed:
they (Papists) are so poor and ignorant that they are not

likely to be consulted on any business by their more wealthy brethren[12].

Perhaps so, but not so poor and ignorant as to be deceived by falsehood. Twenty years before Emancipation, A Plain Blunt Man wrote in Walter Cox's *Irish Magazine* and *Monthly Asylum of Neglected Biography*, 25 March 1808:

> I have always had my fears of the intentions of the Dublin Catholic aristocracy, and I am, by recent occurrences, fully persuaded that they are only struggling hard with each other to try who can bring us first to market. In fact the natural representatives of the people by their self-appointment, their insolent assumption of an exclusive right of leadership, ought to excite our indignation and make us cast them from our confidence . . . etc.[13]

Six years later, in March 1814, a writer asked, in a letter addressed 'to the people of Carlow' – again in the irrepressible Cox's magazine:

> What have we to expect from the higher order of Catholics should they be emancipated? How melancholy to reflect, that whenever they get into power, they uniformly become the tools of any despot, and the oppressors of those who have the misfortune to fall under their government. They sometimes wonder at the indifference the people manifest at their emancipation; but can they be otherwise than indifferent to the fate of men, who have been always the first to betray them?[14]

More than fifty years later, in 1866, the universally respected W. K. Sullivan bore unconscious witness to the perception of these two commentators:

> The few Catholic noblemen and wealthy commons connected with Ireland, emancipated *by the sacrifices of Irish peasants*, have retired into the peaceable enjoyment of the social equality thus won for them, and exert no influence whatever upon Catholic affairs or Irish public opinion.[15]

Not only had they betrayed their beggared compatriots however, in many cases they had defected from the ancient faith. Ambrose Coleman OP drew attention to this fact in 1892:

27

Judging merely by numbers, the Catholics, during the latter half of the (eighteenth) century, made wonderful progress; and while they increased year by year, there was an absolute decrease among the Protestants. But this triumphal progress was counter-balanced in many ways by evils of great magnitude and far-reaching results; so great, indeed, that thoughtful men of the time considered it rather a period of decline than a period of progress.[16]

The reasons adduced by Coleman for this turn of events may be stated briefly:

(a) Because of social intercourse with Protestants of the upper class (and of materialistic philosophy) religious indifference made rapid strides among upper-class Catholics, particularly since the penal laws, so long a barrier between the two, no longer functioned *de jure*, whatever about the reality![17]

(b) As a consequence, such families no longer considered the priesthood a desirable vocation for their sons so that the supply and support of the clergy fell on the middle and lower classes[18].

The sons of such families were not slow to take the signals proffered by parents who were already apostatizing, not because of the penal laws but precisely because such laws no longer pressed upon them:

Their wealth went to satisfy the claims of fashionable society; and while it went in that way, there grew up in their hearts a secret contempt for the poverty, and, to their eyes, vulgarity, of the Church in which they were reared.[19]

The change in such people became quickly evident in the legal profession where Catholics began to make ground late in the eighteenthth century, as Watty Cox remarked in respect of "Catholic Lawyers" – with a trace of his customary asperity. "This description of persons is becoming very numerous[20]," he said derisively, and went on to describe graphically the self-importance he observed, even in the barber's shop, in young Roman Catholic lawyers – probably the first profession to be re-inhabited by members of the old religion:

As soon as the young lawyer is mounted by his barber he . . . throws off all recollection of the peasant life, or the industrious counter which he started from – is transformed into an Aristocrat, and in a moment, discovers that Popery "is not suited to a gentleman . . ."[21]

The reader will note Cox's calculated association of 'the peasant life' with 'the industrious counter', that is, the trading counter of the lower class merchants. It is once again O'Sullivan Béarra's dismissive identification of 'merchants' and 'plebians'. Meanwhile the professional Roman Catholic lawyer had arrived!

What could one have expected from the children of such parents, the *novi homines* and the neo-professionals who were so quick to shed the old allegiance to the faith? The answer was given in a letter in each of three successive months, July, August and September 1809, in *Cox's Magazine*. In July of that year appeared the first of these letters, written by a visiting English Roman Catholic who signed himself *Papista*, and addressed "To the Rev. Gentlemen of Denmark-street Chapel":

> At the solemn offering of the Mass . . . in your chapel we see a crowd on every Sunday of frivolous, foolish coxcombs, studiously mirthful, offensively prying into the faces of every female, indecently chattering to each other and refusing to bend their knee during the solemn sacrifice.[22]

Papista was careful to note that these were not poor people but
> a number of what are called *gentlemen*, standing grinning and buffooning, whilst they (the poor) are prostrate adoring their Redeemer . . . I never see one of them give a penny at the door. I have also watched and observed that on a day that there is a charity sermon in your chapel, when the call upon them is the more marked, they all stay away.[23]

Finally,
> in Liffey-street and Denmark-street chapels there is a scandalous indecency which no chapel in the city has ever witnessed.[24]

Papista's second letter, addressed to the same 'Rev. Gentlemen' appeared in *Cox's Magazine*, in August, 1809. The writer was profoundly annoyed because
> a swarm of rich puppies and well-dressed beggars, repeatedly by their ill manners and scandalous levity gave occasion to that

great and revered character, Doctor Clarke of Liffey-street, to rebuke them.[25]

He felt that, among Roman Catholics, not only professional families were reneging on the old allegiance but the trading or commercial classes as well:

> who have suddenly popped into fortunes that they are not able to bear. Their fathers, illiterate, oppressed and insulted people . . . made sudden fortunes . . . cringing to their superiors and revenging it by trampling on everyone with less money than they possessed . . . Hence have we a spawn of Catholic puppyism unmatched anywhere, who seem to have made a select committee in your chapel.[26]

The third letter of this "honest English Roman Catholic" was published by Watty Cox in September 1809. *Papista* had been staying in a hotel and "a young gentleman" had taken him to "the most fashionable chapel in Dublin." He has left us a memorable account of the swanky portion of the congregation who attended Mass in Denmark St. As for the youth who piloted him there:

> He was the son of a rich merchant who from the lowest species had acquired a real fortune, his father from some feeling which I learn is too general among the Irish, imagined that the farther he was educated from where he himself was not educated, the better gentleman would he make his son, and the more would he find him accomplished.[27]

Papista summed him up briefly and mercilessly:

> he is worth a vast deal of money, belongs to the first mercantile house in town and was dressed to the utmost point of elegance. He had a most sneering, malevolent turn . . .[28]

The juxtaposition of elegance and sneering malevolence seems deliberately contrived. More plausible is the fact that the failure to pass on the faith is attributed not only to the new professional class, as Watty Cox appeared at first to suggest in treating of lawyers, but also to the *boni homines*, the successful mercantile traders whose background was so often one of pinching poverty and little or no schooling but whose lust for money knew no bounds.

It is but fair to point out that *Papista*, the visiting English

30

Catholic is our only witness to all the scenes touched on above. There is a ring of observed truth about them all however – time, place and circumstance are carefully noted – and if any objections were raised in respect of them Cox left them unpublished. It may be noted too that James Berry, honest and acute observer of the small farmers of Connaught, noted that "the rich peasantry of their day (eighteenth century) affected the garb of the Upper Ten."[29] Even the blind Northern poet, James Mac Cuarta (c.1660?-1733), felt called on to satirise an ignoramus who chose to show off his expensive clothes at Mass. The first of sixteen verses will suffice to show the uncompromising bitterness of the blind man who did not, of course, see the one of whom he disapproved but who must have heard the neighbours complain and who sought to humiliate the upstart by questioning his education:

> Answer my question, loud-mouth,
> posturing brash and bravely,
> straight fornent the altar:
> did ye go far in the books?[30]

Finally, while still on the subject of expensive clothes we may risk a paragraph from a letter to the *Dublin Evening Post,* dated July 30th, 1778, one of many from the quill of the redoubtable Amyas Griffith and one that offers the clearest evidence of the almost unnatural concern of the people with the manner of their dress:

> To such a vast height is our military disposition arrived, that incredible numbers of Papists are every day recanting in this province (Munster), in order to get into different associations and to be entitled to dress and walk *à la militaire*; and upon my honour I but the other day mistook a taylor for a certain lieutenent-colonel . . . It is really astonishing to see quondam ragged wretches, who would formerly no more wear ruffles and cue-wigs than they'd wear halters, now strutting in regimentals, swords or bayonet, tailed wig, edged ruffles, &c., &c.

And what, it may be asked, has all of this to do with Edmund Rice? Since he was essentially and by choice a most successful money-making merchant and a child of the eighteenth century, certain things might reasonably have been expected of him if the

31

reflection on the offspring of contemporary 'rich merchants' and 'mercantile houses' by the visiting *Papista* warrants any serious interest. One would expect that he be self-centred and contemptuous, that he show minimal interest in matters religious and that in manner, bearing and general conduct he would leave as much to be desired as did those observed by *Papista*. Such an account is scarcely in harmony with the life-style commonly associated with Edmund Rice: regular attendance at Mass for example – possibly even daily Mass – frequent reception of the Eucharist, devotion to the rosary, a practical and increasing sympathy for the poor, and so on. Now it is received doctrine that like the rich young man in the Gospel, all of these things had been done from his youth by the young man from Callan. Is there any good reason to question the absolute truth of this?

Edmund Rice – the one with whom we are familiar – is not known to have had any discernible human blemishes worth commenting on. Surely he was one born to the straight and narrow? In fact there can be no question whatever that the universal and unvarying tradition in Waterford and, strangely enough, in Callan itself seventy years after his death, was that he was a man *raised up, sent* to them by God.[31] One can scarcely avoid the question: if that be so, wherein was he like the rest of us? It merits consideration and comment. There were, after all, two clearly separate and discernible periods in his life: 1762 to 1802, the years in which he grew to manhood and pursued his chosen avocation, and 1802 to 1844, during which years he concerned himself with his religious apostolate. Life is rarely as simple as this, however, and some niggling questions merit our attention.

Can we be sure he was so different from "the frivolous coxcombs" in Denmark St. chapel, "indecently chattering" during Mass? Had he anything in common with "the swarm of rich puppies" who expressly avoided charity sermons and never gave "a penny at the door?" Did he ever display "the ill manners and scandalous levity" peculiar to the "spawn of Catholic puppyism" so bitterly decribed by *Papista*? These were, I repeat, people not unlike him in many ways: young merchant dealers, on the make, in the money, often away from home for days at a time and – dare we suggest it. – lusting for more money, wealth, prestige and the trappings that accompany these pursuits. Most students of the life of Edmund Rice will claim that merely to name such propositions is, almost by that fact alone, to have answered them. But is it? Are we sure that Edmund Rice was never that kind? Are we sure he was always a man of exemplary life? Or can there have been a time when he was at least tempted to follow a broader way? And is it an act of unfilial or unfraternal disloyalty to call in question the virtually untarnished image of him that we have for so long assumed to be his by right?

We may recall that there were two incidents in his life, of each of which an account has already been published, touching his otherwise apparently exemplary character, and that neither of them, to my knowledge, has been subjected to even a cursory scrutiny. Some purpose might be served in holding them up to the light, if only momentarily, as I propose to do.

On May 30, 1863, less than twenty years after the death of Brother Rice, Sir Charles Gavan Duffy carried, in the *Victorian*, a Sydney newspaper of which he was editor, an account of an incident which is related as follows by Br. M. C. Normoyle in *A Tree is Planted*, pp 26,27:

> One day on a visit to Callan and attending Mass in the parish church he (Edmund Rice) was inattentive and appeared distracted. His conduct was considered disedifying. After Mass an old poet, James Phelan of Coolagh, Callan, met young Rice and chided him for his misconduct in the chapel. He told him that his attitude in the House of God was unbecoming of a Catholic. Young Rice took the admonition to heart, and it is thought that the remarks had a very steadying effect on him.

The problems confronting us in a consideration of this incident may be expanded as follows:

1. What precisely did Gavan Duffy or his assistant write? Unfortunately we have no reason to believe that the above extract is, or is not, a quotation from his newspaper nor, if it is merely a summary, are we entirely certain of its accuracy or completeness. Duffy's own account may very well have been a more pungent record of the incident. Did he give a source for the story? If so what was it? After all Edmund Rice was already almost twenty years dead at the time of its publication in 1863, and the incident may have occurred – if it occurred at all – as many as eighty years,

or even more, before its publication. In referring to the incident I have used the expression 'young Rice': the reader will note that Duffy used it twice in the *Victorian*. In brief therefore we cannot comment in a worthwhile fashion on young Rice's behaviour in Callan church until and unless we get, verbatim, Duffy's account – or the one given him – as he left it. It would be of some service, moreover, to feel assured that no subsequent number of the *Victorian* carried further comment, correction, extension or addition that might challenge or alter materially our perception of the incident.

2. As it stands therefore the story is poorly accredited, and flawed accordingly, but possibly true for all that, particularly in view of what *Papista* has to say concerning young merchants in Dublin some years later and their very questionable conduct during Mass. The same disrespect for the Mass is described with a sense of deep outrage in some Irish sermons[32] of the period that have come down to us. What is more, there is a long-standing tradition of disapproval of people flaunting expensive clothes in Irish country churches during Mass (probably in the galleries which were at that time reserved for those who could afford to pay for a seat in them). Even blind poets – Séamas Dall Mac Cuarta (as we have seen) and Raftery – passed unfavourable comment on such vanity. There is clear evidence that this propaganda was aimed at encouraging those people to attend Mass whose clothes were often little better than rags. Whatever about Mac Cuarta, the songs of the almost naked Raftery had an influence over the peasantry in the West of Ireland that no modern propaganda machine could hope to challenge – and it lasted longer.

3. The story at first sight appears to have been recounted with subtle intent to reflect credit on young Rice or to mark his conversion. However, the suggestion that he was "inattentive and appeared distracted" during Mass seems so charmingly inoffensive and appealingly human that only a very naive reader could fail to see through the whitewash. Would inattention and distraction be accounted "disedifying . . . misconduct" of such an order as to call for public disapproval? With every respect for the youth from Callan it seems to me that, if the episode is based on fact, somebody has prepared for us a bland and colourless résumé of a

Sunday morning encounter that gave serious offence to some, at least, of the people of Callan. Such a stand-off as we read of in this story, however soft-pedalled the memory may be, is not common in Irish churches. In fact it is almost unheard-of. Strangely enough however, *Papista* would have recognised it for what it looks like having been: an all-too-familiar experience in churches frequented by young bucks and financial upstarts. It may well have been due to this incident – if it ever happened – that "in his early years . . . it had been stated he (Rice) was too fastidious about dress."[33] Unfortunately, no source is cited for this interesting observation which, if it be true, would appear to indicate that in one way at least the Kilkenny youth was typical of his day.

Lest we come too readily to conclusions, however, I should confess that I have not yet encountered the name James Phelan (the poet of the chapel skirmish) or any other poet named Phelan in any Callan literature known to me. I refer, in the main, to what has been published of O'Sullivan's diary, poems and other writings,[34] to Dáithí Ó hÓgáin's *Duanaire Osraí*[35] and (with much less confidence) to John Prim's Collection which is housed in the Department of Folklore in University College, Dublin.[36] Having admitted which, I should observe, that if the story of Edmund and the poet Phelan are apocryphal, all we read in folklore bears witness to the assurance that the storyteller would certainly have chosen the name of a very well-known poet and attached the tale firmly to him rather than to an anonymous nobody – witness the endless verses and anecdotes associated, apocryphally for the most part, with Eoghan Rua, Aogán Ó Rathaile, Raftery, Cathal Buí and the rest! The fact that such a name was not invoked to perpetuate the incident of *young* Rice, the trouble-maker, is some small particle of evidence that the incident may, after all, be factual. Moreover, it is hard to account for the survival of such a trivial anecdote from, say 1783, when Edmund Rice was twenty one, to 1863 – eighty years later – unless there was some substance to the incident.

For all that, the evidence seems to me to be insufficient. It is much too tenuous: it wants detail and corroboration, a trustworthy source or an established carrier. By this latter I mean the one or more who 'carried' the story for eighty odd years from Phelan in Callan down to Duffy in Sydney. Moreover, the evidence for the defence far outweighs it, as we shall see.

The second reference to Edmund Rice's past that calls for comment is altogether more interesting, although less specific even than Duffy's 'incident', and it is almost never adverted to. It concerns the admirable Maurice Lenihan, the nature of whose relationship with Edmund Rice it is essential to establish first, however little we know of it. Maurice Lenihan was born in Waterford in 1811[37] and was educated at St Patrick's College, Carlow. He is probably best known as the author of *The History of Limerick* which he published by private subscription in 1866. With the encouragement of O'Connell he founded *The Tipperary Vindicator* in 1844, the year of Edmund Rice's death, and was its first editor. In later years he became a member of the Royal Irish Academy and was elected Mayor of Limerick. Fortunately we are informed by the editor of *Memories of Edmund Rice* that "he was secretary to the Temperance Society founded in Mount Sion, and a close friend of Edmund Rice,"[38] but the origin or nature of their relationship is not touched upon nor does the editor mention a source for the important information that they were 'close friends'. Lenihan's name does not appear in the General Index to *A Tree is Planted*.

If we are to judge by the received dates of birth of both men Edmund Rice was 49 years old when Lenihan was born and the latter was 33 when Br. Rice died. Hence there stood half a century between them. Nevertheless Lenihan could publicly assert that he had "had opportunities of knowing and appreciating his (Rice's) exalted worth."[39] Mr. Rice's life was, he said, one "with which we happen to be familiar since our earliest childhood[40]". My own italicised portion of this assertion calls for some definition and explanation. Readers are free to define "our earliest childhood" as they think fit. I believe it is most unlikely to mean that Lenihan had attended school in Mount Sion at any time or for any length of time. He may well have done so but I know of no evidence that he did. He was educated in St Patrick's, Carlow. Michael Quane, in one of his many revealing studies of eighteenth century schools, has assured us that

> it was generally felt that the acceptance of free education involved a stigma of poverty, and most parents, even those about on or just above the poverty line, sent their children to 'pay' schools, which was the description of the vast majority of the schools in Waterford in 1824.[41]

In this regard he referred expressly to the new free schools of the Presentation Sisters and Christian Brothers in that town. Despite the excellence of Michael Quane's research, however, I am unsure that the scene in Waterford has been accurately described. Touching Edmund Rice's work in Mount Sion, Patrick Buggy, a Waterford solicitor wrote in 1912:

> His labours were immediately crowned with success, for after a very few years, my said grand-uncle told me, the better class of Catholics were so impressed with the education given to the poorer class of boys that first attended Br. Rice's schools, that they took their children from the lay academies that were then common, and sent them to the Christian Brothers to get a sound Catholic National education.[42]

In any case I am unsure whether Lenihan ever attended Mount Sion, even briefly, assuming it was convenient for him to do so. Moreover it appears to me that 'earliest childhood' pre-dates any formal schooling, especially in the early nineteenth century. I believe one has to envisage a very young child being presented by its father or mother to an old friend – to Mr. Rice – in which case they must be presumed to have visited Mr. Rice socially, or he them. Should that be so, Maurice Lenihan may possibly have lived in the vicinity of Ballybricken or perhaps in Dunmore, the beautiful seaside resort occasionally visited by Mr. Rice. The matter does not warrant research but I think we may rest assured that, assuming Maurice Lenihan became in later years secretary to the Mount Sion Temperance Society, as Br. Normoyle asserts, he might easily have developed a close relationship with Brother Rice, indeed he virtually claims as much. That he was profoundly moved – and I use the expression only after much deliberation – by the older man's achievements, character and spirit, he leaves us in no doubt. In view of what Lenihan said later, this assurance is of the greatest importance for he was a writer by profession and must be presumed to have expressed himself with clarity. He was not accustomed to hyphenating clauses and phrases when fullstops and commas are the norm, but the opening paragraph of his extraordinary encomium, the first published in a newspaper after the death of Edmund Rice, and by far the longest, is a series of such hyphens, indicating, I believe, that the writer was swept along in a torrent of giddy conviction:

A Man Raised Up

The Waterford papers announce the death of a venerable, a good, and, in the best sense of the word, a great man – a man of powerful mind – of vast knowledge of human nature – of a comprehensive grasp of intellect – of undaunted courage – of irresistible perseverance – of unbending integrity – of pure piety – of immense charity – Edmund Rice, the founder of the Christian Schools – the herald of a new age to Irishmen in the way of instruction – the harbinger of virtue and of blessings – the benefactor of the species, not only in Ireland, but in whatever quarter of the globe the present generation of the humbler classes of our fellow-countrymen have penetrated, because to Mr. Rice is mainly attributable whatever intellectual training they enjoy.[43]

We have had opportunities of knowing and appreciating his exalted worth – of witnessing in some degree the extent and value of his labours – of being partially acquainted with the strength and depth of the magnificent edifice which he raised for the instruction of the children of the poor of his native city in the first instance, and of Ireland, almost universally, afterwards.[44]

He regretted, not without bitterness, "that those who are on the spot (i.e. in Lenihan's own town, Waterford) have not been able to contribute more particulars of the life and exertions of "this truly excellent man."[45] He was himself "not exactly informed of the causes that operated on the mind of Mr. Rice" to take the step he had taken in founding the Brotherhood.[46] Then, with little apparent reason for doing so, Lenihan made a single short, simple statement challenging us for what it may imply and tantalising us for what it leaves unsaid:

We believe that Mr. Rice's early life had not given promise of that religious earnestness which he now (c.1798?) began to display.[47]

The range of possibilities opened up by this strange aside of Maurice Lenihan, coming as it does in a sweep of heartfelt adulation may, in itself, be sufficient reason for the failure of commentators to seek to divine its purpose or probable meaning.

To anyone familiar with the standard account of the virtuous life of Edmund Rice and the profound respect of Maurice Lenihan for him, the statement comes as a hammer-blow. Where did Lenihan hear it? Why is it the only suggestion of its kind in 270 contributions to *Memories*? Most people will feel the impact of it even before they have carefully studied its implications. Bearing in mind that Edmund Rice was almost fifty years older than Lenihan, the latter can have heard the story – whatever it was – only from people considerably older than himself and who, if they were friends of Lenihan, almost certainly loved and revered Br. Rice. The statement, we note, is negative: Mr. Rice's early life "had not given promise." It may indeed be entirely innocuous but if so why insert it into a death-notice, especially one of such a laudatory nature? Is it not a common human reaction, when one is told that so-and-so was not always of a given way of thinking or acting, to assume that he was almost certainly of another way of behaving? In plain truth, does it not really mean that he was not then the man of God he became later in life? Only gradually does the force – the menace? – of the opening phrase touch us: "We believe" this to have been the case! As who should say, "it is hard to believe, but the well-kept secret is . . ." Otherwise why not remark casually: "No more than any young man, Mr Rice did/did not . . ."

Whatever the unspoken alternative to "religious earnestness" may have been it seems clear that Lenihan felt it best not to name it! All the same he appears to have judged it to be the life-style from which young Rice, to his great credit, turned away.

To the reader belongs the choice of deciding whether or not there is in Lenihan's casual remark an unsubtle suggestion that Edmund Rice had, in his earlier years, developed a reputation not too dissimilar to that described so vividly by *Papista* in Dublin, only a few years after the opening of Mount Sion, and relating expressly to immature young merchants. Indeed it differs not a great deal from the thinly-veiled accusation of Phelan, the poet, in Callan, also in the early years of Edmund's business life. There is no doubt that both memories are of a piece – more especially if Lenihan's comment has been correctly interpreted. If not however, and assuming Lenihan means literally what he says, one wonders why he said it at all for it means no more than that Edmund Rice devoted himself to his business with an intensity unbecoming a christian young man. Would such a commonplace experience have remained so long in the memory of older people as to be passed on to a generation fifty years younger? And if so would it have been a comment suited to a death notice redolent of a deep personal respect? At any rate it cannot be said to justify the nuance perceived by this reader, at least, in the menacing assurance 'we believe' – as though it were some old and carefully-hidden secret that might now at last be whispered.

Finally it may be argued that the expression 'religious earnestness' is so indefinite as to make it worthless, for it is certainly insufficient evidence to induce us to believe that the young man had become brazenly irreligious in the way *Papista* had seen in Dublin churches and described for us. To balance that, I may conclude by suggesting that since the older folk who had known Edmund Rice as a young man are most likely to have been the source of Lenihan's information and since these older people, if they were friends of Lenihan were most probably friends and admirers of Br. Rice, as most people who knew him appear to have been in his advancing years, then we are justified in assuming that any comments of an unfavourable kind made by them concerning their old and admired friend are very likely to have been made *sotto voce*, much as they remained *sotto voce* in respect of everything related to his young wife – even her name, surname and religious persuasion. One never ceases wondering why?[48]

This observation leads in turn to a further intriguing question: why did no other among the 270 testimonies in *Memories* bear witness to an earlier and possibly less admirable life-style known to have been embraced by Edmund– Rice – if indeed it had been? In seeking to find an answer to this problem I dismissed for the moment the Waterford evidence and turned to what the people of Callan had to say because, to Callan, after all, is referred the incident recalled or invented by Gavan Duffy and possibly even that to which Lenihan referred. And here a remarkable phenomenon may be observed. Of 249 personal submissions (there are 21 others from newspapers) recorded in *Memories of Edmund Rice*, 32 are from Callan, the hometown of Edmund. Now these memories, recorded in Callan, offer evidence that is quite remarkable for this reason: the Rices, as a group, and Edmund, personally, are invariably spoken about in depositions from Callan in terms of the most genuine respect, bordering at times almost on adulation, but, touching both the extended family and the man himself, one single human weakness is named repeatedly and attributed both to them and to Edmund in person. There is never an indication that the deponents enjoyed doing so but neither is there ever a suggestion that they pulled punches. They spoke the truth as they saw it without a trace of venom or spite or a suggestion that this was their opportunity to besmirch the fair name of a saintly man or the family whose name he bore and who were well worthy of him, as he, indeed, of them.

With the extended family of the Rices we are not concerned here, nor even with the matured merchant whose decision changed the face of Waterford. The *youthful* Edmund Rice is our concern here and, touching his character, as it was known and remembered in Callan, we are left in no doubt. The following selection of depositions, all of which refer only to the young Edmund Rice, are from Callan:

Thomas Murphy knew James Stapleton who was born in Callan c.1762, the year of Edmund Rice's own birth. He said that
Br. Rice as a young man, was very good. He was first educated in his own house and that (*sic*) he bore an excellent character.[49]

Mrs O'Grady of Westcourt, Callan, heard her father and father-in-law (both born before 1812) say that
Br. Rice, when young, was a very good young man . . . From the goodness of his early life they were not in the least astonished that he turned out so well . . . This was . . . the belief of the people of the neighbourhood who were familiar with Br. Rice in his early days.[50]

Martin Ryan, "a native of Callan" deposed that
It was said amongst the people that (Edmund Rice) from his youth upwards had an inclination towards piety. I heard the people say that since he was a boy barely able to walk, he frequented Holy Mass in the Augustinian Church of Callan.[51]

Johanna Murphy, Westcourt, Callan recalled her father speak of
Br. Rice as being a holy and religious person always. He had learned this from his own father who would be a young man

at the time Br. Rice was a young man. This testimony of my father and grandfather which I learned as I have stated is fresh in my memory today. From the good things handed down to me about Edmund Rice in regard to his young days I have no doubt that he was a pious and saintly man.[52]

Of all the respondents to the request to record memories of Edmund Rice, few impressed the first collector, Br. Mark Hill, as did Mary O'Reilly of Carrick-on-Suir, a lady who observed, recalled and wrote, not without distinction. She had

heard it said of him that he was holy from his youth up.[53]

We may note finally that a man born in Waterford about 1830 remarked that

Br. Rice had the name of having a religious turn when he came to Waterford as a *young man*. In fact he was credited with having a religious turn *from his cradle*.[54]

There is no lack of evidence therefore pointing to the goodness and virtue of young Edmund Rice long before he left Callan nor have we begun to exhaust the evidence. Strangely, one never gets the feeling that people spoke in this way merely because they were expected to do so. What is remarkable is, not that they named clearly the only fault thought to be characteristic of the Rices, but that those who did so invariably spoke most impressively indeed of the excellence of that family despite its human defect. Edmund too was seen to have a weakness and people could hardly doubt what it was – he shared it with the Rices:

I recollect some old people saying that the Rices were ambitious for land and were anxious to get rich quickly.[55]

The Rices were considered to have been perhaps, endowed by a too keen sense of business.[56]

They (Rices) were fond of land and were always anxious to secure a good place.[57]

Only one Rice however was thought to be responsible (in *Memories*) for the eviction of a tenant from a rented holding. The account is that of Thomas Heron whose family, in 1912, were in Callan for three hundred years. No person who knew the Rices at close range thought so well of them or spoke so highly as did Thomas Heron. Yet he did not feel constrained to hide what he felt was the truth:

> Land was a big source of trouble here long ago, and indeed up to recent years. Those who had the money, occasionally bought or rented holdings from which tenants were evicted or broke for one reason or another. I heard some old people refer to the fact that Edmund Rice took farms which some less prosperous people were unable to hold. He re-set these farms and from the proceeds financed his schools. Some of the descendants of the people who thus lost their holdings in the Minauns area of Callan, were rather critical of and embittered against Br. Rice. I heard that in the Minauns he took the holdings of the following families: O'Leary, Ard, Walsh, Murphy, Roughan.
>
> Outside the question of Edmund Rice and the land I never heard anything but the very best of him. Indeed, his work was praised and his memory blessed by the older generation.[58]

Since the people of Callan were clearly unafraid to speak their minds (in 1912-13, when most of the depositions quoted above were taken) there seems to be no good reason why a skirmish at a church door would not be recalled, had there ever been such – though Sydney is a long way to go for such an account just as eighty years was a long time to await its publication! Nobody in Callan appears to have heard of the fracas, and it is a matter for the reader to assess the likelihood of its ever having happened. When such a scene did occur at the church door in Callan in 1808, though not in association with a parish Mass, the incident immediately called forth a ballad in praise of Fr. Millea, the Parish Priest who fought his attackers with his bare fists. Nobody made a ballad for Edmund's fastidious dress – not even Phelan, the untraceable poet who was part of the shenanigan.

On the other hand there is every likelihood that the story of Edmund's covetousness to possess as much land as possible, may well have been remembered and would almost certainly have become known in Waterford where Callan folk frequently met and re-lived the past. After all, he was never a man to do things by halves. The problem abides.

A Man Raised Up

Postscript

Since we have been scrutinising the conduct of Edmund Rice in the context of his time, it may be well to remark, by way of conclusion, that when he opted for the vocation to the classroom, however fancifully we may name it, he chose, knowingly and with deliberation aforethought, what was felt to be the least of all professions in his day, for most teachers at that time were physically handicapped in some way as O'Rorke remarked in his *History of Sligo* (c. 1889):

> the schoolmasters of one hundred years ago suffered common-ly from some weighty physical defect – they being in many cases hunchbacks, cripples, or victims of some such bodily affliction.[59]

O'Rorke believed that, since 'school' was so often conducted in a wet and dirty ditch and was moreover forbidden by law, only the weakest would make application for the 'privilege' of teaching.[60] One can but marvel at the selfless decision of a successful and ambitious man, such as Edmund Rice undoubtedly was, to opt, in faith, for a calling that was not only forbidden and poorly paid but was felt moreover to be suited only to the crippled and the handicapped.

References

1 *Comhairle Mhic Clamha*, ed. by Seosamh Dufaigh

2 *Commissarius na Cléire*, ed. by Seosamh Dufaigh in *Studia Hibernica*, No. 7

3 *Pairlement Chloinne Tomáis* ed. by N. J. A. Williams, Dublin Institute for Advanced Studies, 1981.

4 *Párliament na mBan* ed. by Brian Ó Cuív. Institiúid Ard-Léinn, BAC

5 *The Life and Death of the Most Reverend Francis Kirwan*, Bishop of Killala. Translated by C. P. Meehan Dublin 1848.

6 Optimates omniae (Galviae)

7 *Irish Ecclesiastical Colleges Since the Reformation*. Santiago. I. E. R., Jan 1874, pp. 167-181. Cf p. 171

8 *The History of the Town and County of Galway*. Dub. 1820. by James Hardiman. Reprinted Galway 1926, p. 322

9 *A Bishop of Penal Times*, by James Coombes. Tower Books of Cork, 1981.

10 ib. Ó Briain was accused of being "one of obscure talents and lineage", and of being "meanly born". Cf. pp 36, 37.

11 *Seanmóirí Muighe Nuadhad*, 1, 187

12 Historical Mss. Commission. Twelfth Report. Appendix, Part X. The Manuscripts and Correspondence of James, First Earl of Charlemont. Vol 1. 1745-83. London 1891. Cf. p. 311

13 *The National Magazine of Neglected Biography*. Italics mine.

14 *The Irish Magazine and Monthly Asylum of Neglected Biography.* March 1814, p. 106, col, b.

15 *University Education in Ireland.* W. K. Sullivan, Dublin 1866. 2nd Ed., p. 27.

16 IER, Vol. X111, 1892, p. 828.

17 ib., p. 829

18 ib.

19 ib.

20 Cox, *The Irish Magazine* 1815 p. 74

21 ib., p. 75.

22 ib., 1809, p. 307-8.

23 ib.

24 ib.

25 ib., p. 349.

26 ib.

27 ib., p. 388

28 ib. 389

29 James Berry: *Tales of the West of Ireland.* Ed. by Gertrude M. Horgan. Dublin, 1966. Second Edition 1969.

30 "Ceist agam ort, a spalpaire." From an unpublished dissertation for MA by Seán Gallchóir. The attribution to Mac Cuarta is doubtful.

31 For examples of this opinion see *Memories* pp. 8, 136, 205, 218, 225, etc.

32 e.g. *Seanmóirí Muighe Nuadhad*, 2, 184-196

33 *A Tree is Planted*, p. 26. No source cited.

34 Michael McGrath sj edited, in four volumes of the Irish Texts Society, Vols XXX-XXXIII, all of the diary of Humphrey O'Sullivan (1780-1838) with a translation and excellent apparatus, together with some further effusions of prose and verse. Professor Tomás de Bhaldraithe edited a much reduced version of the diary, *Cín Lae Amhlaoibh*, published by An Clóchomhar in 1970. He noted that many of O'Sullivan's writings remain yet to be published. Because the latter, a schoolmaster who occasionally turned shopkeeper, spent most of his life in Callan, he is commemorated by a plaque on the front wall of the house in which he lived (not more than a 100 yards from the statue of Edmund Rice). Since the two men were contemporaries, Edmund Rice being the older by 18 years, it is high time O'Sullivan's work was scrutinised for what it may contain that could shed light on the Rices of Callan. This is particularly true in respect of his unpublished manuscripts, however jejune, to which our attention was drawn by Professor de Bhaldraithe.

35 A collection of Irish poems, mostly 18th and 19th century, from the barony of Ossory – Edmund Rice country – published by An Clóchomhar, 1980. Much of it is taken from the Prim Collection. See next note.

36 The Prim Collection comprises six boxes of folklore, songs, ballads, and various anecdotes from the eighteenth and early nineteenth centuries collected in the Callan area at the request of John Prim in the mid-nineteenth century. It was bequeathed to the Irish Folklore Commission, forerunner to the Department of Folklore in UCD. Both Br. W. B. Cullen and myself trawled the collection in the 1960s and some of it has since then been published by Dr. Daithí Ó hÓgáin. See previous note.

37 Maurice Lenihan born 5 Feb. 1811, died Christmas Day, 1895. Educated St. Patrick's College, Carlow, associated with *The Tipperary Free Press* (1831), *The Waterford Chronicle* (Editor 1833-34), *The Limerick Reporter* (Editor1834-43), and *The Tipperary Vindicator* (Founder and Editor 1844). His magnum opus, *Limerick, Its History and Antiquities* was published in 1866. His Reminiscences appeared in the *Limerick Reporter* 1866-69 but never appeared in book form. Foregoing from Henry Boylan's *A Dictionary of Irish Biography*, Dublin 1978.

38 *Memories*, p. 297, note 1.

39 ib., p. 332
40 ib., p. 343
41 Michael Quane: Waterford Schools in the Opening Decades of the Nineteenth Century. JRSAI 101: 141-143.
42 *Memories*, pp. 331-32
43 ib., 332.
44 ib.
45 ib., 333
46 I have dealt with this in some detail in an essay "The Call of Edmund Rice", the publication of which is long overdue.
47 *Memories*, p. 333
48 See "The Death of Mrs. Rice."
49 *Memories* p. 205
50 ib., p. 225
51 ib., 180
52 ib., 202
53 ib., 227
54 ib.,121
55 ib., 114-15
56 ib., 138
57 ib., 253
58 ib.
59 *The History of Sligo: Town and County*. T. O'Rorke, Dublin n.d. (1889), Vol 2, p. 443
60 ib.

Aspects of Rice Family History[1]

J. Matthew Feheney, PFM

IN MAY 1990 I got a strange and unexpected telephone call from Melbourne, Australia. The caller was Joe Rice who informed me that he was coming to Ireland and wanted me to give him some help in tracing his forbears. He mentioned that there was a story in his family that he was related to Edmund Rice, founder of the Presentation and Christian Brothers. At a later stage Joe cited a story that his grandfather told his eldest brother that he was *"a relative of the Rice man who founded the Christian Brothers."*[2]

In June 1990 Joe, then well into his eighties, flew from Australia to Cork, accompanied by his daughter, specifically to unravel the secrets of his family history. I think it would be true to say that this quest was increasingly occupying his time. Over a meal he told me the following story.

His grandfather, Robert Rice, born in Cork 1833, was the son of Robert Rice and Jane Wright. The family tradition was that young Robert's uncle, who was connected with shipping in Waterford, "put him on a cargo boat and sent him to Australia". Joe has no doubts about the story so far. The next part of Joe's story was surmise: that the Cork Robert Rice, married to Jane Wright, mainly because he had a brother connected with shipping in Waterford, was related to Robert Rice, Edmund's father, of Callan. This article is essentially a report of the investigation set in motion by Joe Rice's telephone call to me in May 1990.

Rice Clan in Cork

Since Joe said that his grandfather came from Cork, I began my investigation there. As his grandfather was supposed to be born in 1833 and sailed from Ireland around 1856, I checked the Cork *Postal Directory*[3] for 1844-45 (the earliest one available in the Cork City Library) and found the following Rices listed:

> John Rice, Woollen draper, 52 Great George Street, Cork
> George Rice, Publican, 39 Barrack Street, Cork
> Howard Rice, Bridewell Keeper, Bridewell, Cork
> Thomas Rice, Chandler, 31 Barrack Street, Cork
> Mrs Betty Rice, 371 Blarney Lane, Cork

There is, however, no mention of a Robert Rice, Flour Miller. Moreover, though Joe's grandfather was, as far as he knows, baptised a Catholic, the probability is that at least some of these Rices, especially Howard Rice, Keeper of the Bridewell, were Protestant.

Next I searched the Baptism Registers of the City parishes for that time. This was not so difficult in view of the fact that there were then only three parishes in Cork City, named, very logically, the North Parish, the South Parish and the Middle Parish. The first thing I noticed was that few Rices were listed in either the Baptism or Marriage Registers; the second was that there was no sign of a Robert Rice born to Robert Rice and Jane Wright in or around 1833. I did, however, find some Rice baptisms. For instance, though the Middle Parish (Ss Peter and Paul) has no record of a Rice marriage between 1828 and 1833, some Rice children were baptised there: Eliza Jane Rice, daughter of John Rice and Catherine Clarke in 1831, and John Rice, son of John Rice and Johanna Cahill, in 1833.[4] The North Parish register for the same period does not record any Rice being married or baptised.

By 1863, however, the number of Rices in Cork, whether Protestant or Catholic, had increased. The *Cork Mercantile Directory*[5] for 1863 lists the following Rices:

Thomas Rice, Corn Merchant, 11 Merchants' Quay, Cork (with residence at Ardarostig)
Robert Rice, Flour Factor, 62 Friar's Walk, Cork
William Rice, Grocer, 92 North Main Street, Cork.

Shortly afterwards (1867), the *Directory for Cork and Munster*[6] lists some more:

Robert Rice, Miller and Grocer, 66 Ballyhooley Road, Cork
C Rice, 6 Evergreen Terrace, Cork
Mrs N Rice, Huckster, 6 Robert Street, Cork
Thomas Rice, Corn Merchant, 11 Merchants' Quay (Residence Wilton), Cork
William Rice, Grocer, 15 North Main Street, Cork

The most promising connection with Joe Rice seemed to be the Robert Rice, Miller and Grocer, at 66 Ballyhooley Road. Joe was insistent that his great grandfather was a flour miller. The next step was to check the addresses of the 31 Rices listed in the current Cork telephone directory to see if any corresponded with the addresses given over one hundred years ago. Again one stood out:66 Ballyhooley Road. In 1867 this was the address of Robert Rice, Miller. At present it is the address of James Rice, whose grandfather was Robert and who has a son Robert Rice, resident at the family farm in Ballinhassig, Co Cork. James, however, is a Protestant, as has been his family for several generations. I did find, however, that more than a century ago, there was a Catholic connection.

Half Family Protestant
The most significant thing about the family of Robert Rice, Miller, from 66 Ballyhooley Road, from a genealogical point of view, was the predominance of the name Robert in almost every generation. The sequence of first names of the Rice family at 66 Ballyhooley Road since the late 1700s was Robert Rice (b. late 1700s), Robert Rice (listed in Directory for Cork and Munster 1867), Robert Rice (b. c.1850 who married Mary Busteed), James Rice (1875-1968, who married Hester Young), James Rice (b. c.1904, married Catherine Cashman), Robert Rice (b. 1950, married Mary Kingston).[7]

The wife of Robert Rice, who was born in the late 1700s, died young and he married again. Since the first wife was Protestant the children from this union were brought up as Protestants (Church of Ireland). The second wife, however, was Catholic and her children were brought up as Catholics. The occurrence of such so called mixed marriages, especially among well-to-do Catholics, was not unusual in Ireland at the time. The result of this second union is that there are two sets of Rice cousins in the Ballinhassig area, one Protestant and the other Catholic.[8]

Like the Callan Rices this Cork branch was prosperous by the standards of the time. In addition to the business in Cork, the family also had a good deal of land in the Ballinhassig area. Griffith's Valuation[9] for 1850 lists Robert Rice, who seems to represent the Protestant branch, as having a lease of 68 acres of land from Daniel Lombard while James Rice, who seems to represent the Catholic branch, is listed as having 137 acres, also leased from Daniel Lombard, at Barrett's Hill, where the family is now resident.

Since, however, there is no family tradition of any connection with Waterford or Callan among the Ballyhooley Road/Ballinhassig Rices, it is unlikely that they are Joe's long lost cousins.

Callan Rices to Cork?

Since it was obviously not the Founder, who died in 1844, who arranged the passage of Robert Rice, the Australian emigrant, in 1855, who could it have been? One possibility is that the passage was arranged by one of Uncle Michael Rice's grandsons. It will be recalled that Uncle Michael had two sons (see accompanying Family Tree, "FT01: Rice Family of Callan"), Patrick and Robert.[10] Joe Rice, himself, suggests that one of these, Robert, was the forbear of Robert the Australian emigrant, and that a son of the other, Patrick, who remained in Waterford, was the person that arranged the passage. This is a distinct possibility: the dates would tally. It is assumed that both Robert and Patrick were approximately the same age as the Founder, who was born 1762. Their children would be born in the late 1780s and their grandchildren in the first decade of the 1800's. So Robert the emigrant could have been a great grandson of Uncle Michael's son, Robert, and a great grand nephew of Patrick.

An examination of the baptism registers of the Waterford churches, while giving information, does not help us to identify the name of this particular Rice man. The entries, which would appear to be most relevant to our inquiry, would seem to be from Ballybricken parish giving the names and dates of baptism of children of Patrick Rice and Eleanor Power, a relative of Bishop John Power, friend of the Founder. The first is a boy, Robert Rice, baptised 29 January, 1798. The next child, a girl, baptised 14 March 1800, was named Alice Rice.[11]

Joe Rice suggests that it was possibly this Robert Rice, baptised 29 January, 1798, who later came to Cork, set up as a flour miller, married Jane Wright and was the father of the Australian emigrant, born 1833.[12] The dates would fit. However, so far the connection is largely surmise and we yet have to find evidence to confirm it.

FT01: Rice Family of Callan
Rhys of Wales(To Ireland 12 th C)

JM Feheney

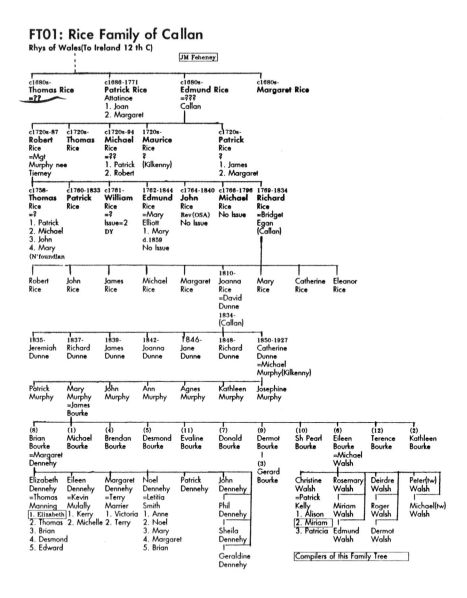

| c1680s- Thomas Rice =?? | c1686-1771 Patrick Rice Attatinoe 1. Joan 2. Margaret | c1680s- Edmund Rice =??? Callan | c1680s- Margaret Rice |

c1720s-87 Robert Rice =Mgt Murphy nee Tierney

c1720s- Thomas Rice

c1720s-94 Michael Rice =?? 1. Patrick 2. Robert

1720s- Maurice Rice (Kilkenny)

c1720s- Patrick Rice ? 1. James 2. Margaret

c1758- Thomas Rice =? 1. Patrick 2. Michael 3. John 4. Mary (N'foundlan

c1760-1833 Patrick Rice

c1761- William Rice =? Issue=2 DY

1762-1844 Edmund Rice =Mary Elliott 1. Mary d.1859 No Issue

c1764-1840 John Rice Rev(OSA) No Issue

c1766-1796 Michael Rice No Issue

1769-1834 Richard Rice =Bridget Egan (Callan)

Robert Rice

John Rice

James Rice

Michael Rice

Margaret Rice

1810- Joanna Rice =David Dunne 1834- (Callan)

Mary Rice

Catherine Rice

Eleanor Rice

1835- Jeremiah Dunne

1837- Richard Dunne

1839- James Dunne

1842- Joanna Dunne

1846- Jane Dunne

1848- Richard Dunne

1850-1927 Catherine Dunne =Michael Murphy(Kilkenny)

Patrick Murphy

Mary Murphy =James Bourke

John Murphy

Ann Murphy

Agnes Murphy

Kathleen Murphy

Josephine Murphy

(8) Brian Bourke =Margaret Dennehy

(1) Michael Bourke

(4) Brendan Bourke

(5) Desmond Bourke

(11) Evaline Bourke

(7) Donald Bourke

(9) Dermot Bourke | (3) Gerard Bourke

(10) Sh Pearl Bourke

(6) Eileen Bourke =Michael Walsh

(12) Terence Bourke

(2) Kathleen Bourke

Elizabeth Dennehy =Thomas Manning 1. Elizabeth 2. Thomas 3. Brian 4. Desmond 5. Edward

Eileen Dennehy =Kevin Mulally 1. Kerry 2. Michelle

Margaret Dennehy =Terry Marrier 1. Victoria 2. Terry

Noel Dennehy =Letitia Smith 1. Anne 2. Noel 3. Mary 4. Margaret 5. Brian

Patrick Dennehy

John Dennehy Phil Dennehy Sheila Dennehy Geraldine Dennehy

Christine Walsh =Patrick Kelly 1. Alison 2. Miriam 3. Patricia

Rosemary Walsh Miriam Walsh Edmund Walsh

Deirdre Walsh Roger Walsh Dermot Walsh

Peter(tw) Walsh Michael(tw) Walsh

Compilers of this Family Tree

51

One of the points to be borne in mind is that it is likely that the Founder had several of his relatives employed with him in his victualler and ship-chandler business. The custom of the time was that members of a family regarded it as a duty to give the younger relatives a start in life. Just as the Founder, himself, was befriended by his uncle Michael, so, he, also, would be expected to promote the prospects of other relatives. Besides, there is the question of compensation for the two sons of Michael Rice, whom the Founder superseded in their father's business. Edmund's scrupulous honesty would prompt him to make suitable remuneration to them, or, perhaps give them shares in the business. The probability, therefore, of other Rice relatives continuing in the victualler and ship-chandler business is high.[13]

Though Joe Rice did not solve the puzzle of his ancestry during his visit to Ireland in 1990 I did put him in contact with several knowledgeable Christian Brothers as well as with a Rice genealogy enthusiast, Bride Roe, of New Ross, Co. Wexford, whose mother was a Rice and whose great-great-great-grandfather was John Rice of Callan. Since Bride, a direct descendant of the Callan Rices, has a personal interest in Rice family history and has assiduously collected family traditions and lore over the years, we will discuss at length some of her findings and theories. Her own family tree is set out in "FT03: Rice Family of New Ross".

New Ross Rices
John Rice, Bride's great-great-great-grandfather, was born in Callan in 1756, and moved to New Ross, Co Wexford, where he established a bacon curing business in Irishtown. Though he took no active part in the 1798 Rebellion in Wexford, humanitarian considerations urged him to give shelter to some women and children in a loft in his house during the battle of New Ross in 1798. They were discovered, dragged forth and killed. John Rice, himself, was also dragged outside his house and a Hessian officer drew his sword to cut off his head. According to family tradition, John grabbed the sword with his teeth and held it fast, refusing to let go, whereon he was dragged down the street and shot at the cross in Irishtown. He is buried in New Ross.[14]

It is worth noting that it was John Rice's compassion and sense of Christian duty to shelter the innocent in danger that led to his death, for there is nothing to suggest that the Wexford, Waterford

FT02: Rice Family of Newfoundland

Norman Rhys of Wales(To Ireland 12 th C)

JM Feheney

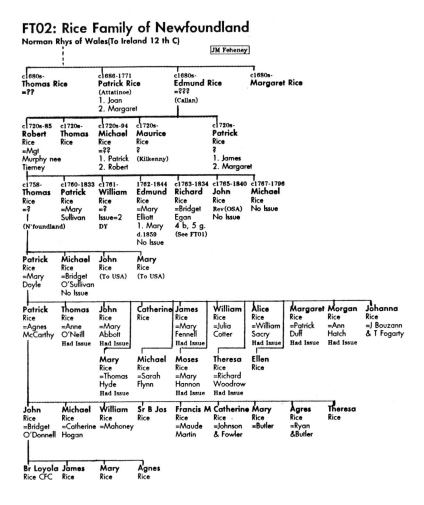

c1680s- **Thomas Rice** =??	c1686-1771 **Patrick Rice** (Attatinoe) 1. Joan 2. Margaret	c1680s- **Edmund Rice** =??? (Callan)	c1680s- **Margaret Rice**

c1720s-85 **Robert** Rice =Mgt Murphy nee Tierney	c1720s- **Thomas** Rice	c1720s-94 **Michael** Rice =?? 1. Patrick 2. Robert	c1720s- **Maurice** Rice ? (Kilkenny)	c1720s- **Patrick** Rice ? 1. James 2. Margaret

c1758- **Thomas** Rice =? (N'foundland)	c1760-1833 **Patrick** Rice =Mary Sullivan	c1761- **William** Rice =? Issue=2 DY	1762-1844 **Edmund** Rice =Mary Elliott 1. Mary d.1859 No Issue	c1763-1834 **Richard** Rice =Bridget Egan 4 b, 5 g. (See FT01)	c1765-1840 **John** Rice Rev(OSA) No Issue	c1767-1796 **Michael** Rice No Issue

Patrick Rice =Mary Doyle	**Michael** Rice =Bridget O'Sullivan No Issue	**John** Rice (To USA)	**Mary** Rice (To USA)

Patrick Rice =Agnes McCarthy	**Thomas** Rice =Anne O'Neill Had Issue	**John** Rice =Mary Abbott Had Issue	**Catherine** Rice	**James** Rice =Mary Fennell Had Issue	**William** Rice =Julia Cotter	**Alice** Rice =William Sacry Had Issue	**Margaret** Rice =Patrick Duff Had Issue	**Morgan** Rice =Ann Hatch Had Issue	**Johanna** Rice =J Bouzann & T Fogarty

Mary Rice =Thomas Hyde Had Issue	**Michael** Rice =Sarah Flynn	**Moses** Rice =Mary Hannon Had Issue	**Theresa** Rice =Richard Woodrow Had Issue	**Ellen** Rice

John Rice =Bridget O'Donnell	**Michael** Rice =Catherine Hogan	**William** Rice =Mahoney	**Sr B Jos** Rice	**Francis M** Rice =Maude Martin	**Catherine** Rice =Johnson & Fowler	**Mary** Rice =Butler	**Agnes** Rice =Ryan &Butler	**Theresa** Rice

Br Loyola Rice CFC	**James** Rice	**Mary** Rice	**Agnes** Rice

and Kilkenny Rices of the period were extreme nationalists. With the sole exception of "The Wild Rapparee", described later, it would be difficult to find evidence of a rebel among them.

John Rice, killed in 1798, was married to Mary Doyle (1777-1857), aunt of the famous Bishop "JKL" Doyle.[15] They had two sons, Michael and John (1790-1886), as well as a daughter, Anastasia.[16]

It has been suggested that John Rice of New Ross may have been a son of the John Rice of Baunlusk, Newlands, mentioned in the will of Patrick Rice of Attatinoe, who died in 1771 and who was a grand uncle of the Founder. This would mean that the New Ross Rices were from the same stock as the Founder.[17] This John Rice is not to be confused with the colourful John Rice, also of Newlands, known locally as "The Wild Rapparee", who was married to the Founder's step-sister, Jane Murphy. An ardent nationalist, he was suspected of being a member of the United Irishmen, a group as famous for the number of patriots it attracted as it was notorious for the number of Government spies that pervaded its council meetings. John's house in Newlands was raided at midnight by a band of local yeomen, who, not finding him at home, proceeded to burn his house, partly as a warning and partly as a punishment. He hid for some time in a quarry nearby until it was safe for him to make his way to Waterford. Here the Founder hid him in his own house until an opportunity came of smuggling him, in a barrel, aboard a vessel bound for Newfoundland.[18]

Though there is no record of this John Rice landing or living in Newfoundland, there are several Rices and their descendants, both Protestant and Catholic(see accompanying Family Tree, "FT02:Rice Family of Newfoundland"). Some of them have preserved a fragment of a ballad about John the "Rapparee", part of which runs as follows:

> From Ballyhale to Slievenamon
> They searched the woods as they went on;
> The corn fields up the Galtymore,
> They searched and searched them o'er and o'er.
>
> The ships and traders at the quay,
> They searched and searched going out to sea.
> But tale nor tidings, trace nor sound
> Of Rice, the rebel, they ne'er found.[19]

FT03: Rice Family of New Ross

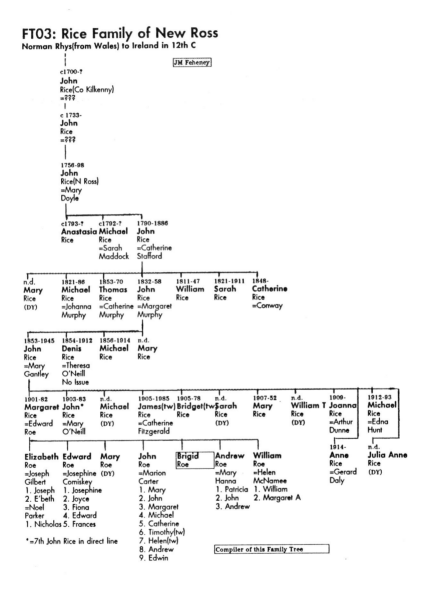

Norman Rhys(from Wales) to Ireland in 12th C

JM Feheney

c1700-?
John
Rice(Co Kilkenny)
=???

c 1733-
John
Rice
=???

1756-98
John
Rice(N Ross)
=Mary
Doyle

c1793-?	c1792-?	1790-1886
Anastasia	**Michael**	**John**
Rice	Rice	Rice
	=Sarah	=Catherine
	Maddock	Stafford

n.d.	1821-86	1853-70	1832-58	1811-47	1821-1911	1848-
Mary	**Michael**	**Thomas**	**John**	**William**	**Sarah**	**Catherine**
Rice	Rice	Rice	Rice	Rice	Rice	Rice
(DY)	=Johanna	=Catherine	=Margaret			=Conway
	Murphy	Murphy	Murphy			

1853-1945	1854-1912	1856-1914	n.d.
John	**Denis**	**Michael**	**Mary**
Rice	Rice	Rice	Rice
=Mary	=Theresa		
Gantley	O'Neill		
	No Issue		

1901-82	1903-83	n.d.	1905-1985	1905-78	n.d.	1907-52	n.d.	1909-	1912-93
Margaret	**John***	**Michael**	**James(tw**	**Bridget(tw**	**Sarah**	**Mary**	**William T**	**Joanna**	**Michael**
Rice	Rice	Rice	Rice	Rice	Rice	Rice	Rice	Rice	Rice
=Edward	=Mary	(DY)	=Catherine		(DY)		(DY)	=Arthur	=Edna
Roe	O'Neill		Fitzgerald					Dunne	Hunt

Elizabeth	Edward	Mary	John	Brigid	Andrew	William	Anne	Julia Anne
Roe	Roe	Roe	Roe	Roe	Roe	Roe	Rice	Rice
=Joseph	=Josephine	(DY)	=Marion		=Mary	=Helen	=Gerard	(DY)
Gilbert	Comiskey		Carter		Hanna	McNamee	Daly	
1. Joseph	1. Josephine		1. Mary		1. Patricia	1. William		
2. E'beth	2. Joyce		2. John		2. John	2. Margaret A		
=Noel	3. Fiona		3. Margaret		3. Andrew			
Parker	4. Edward		4. Michael					
1. Nicholas	5. Frances		5. Catherine					
			6. Timothy(tw)					
*=7th John Rice in direct line			7. Helen(tw)					
			8. Andrew		Compiler of this Family Tree			
			9. Edwin					

1814-
Anne

55

Among the Rice diaspora in Newfoundland are the descendants of the Founder's brother Thomas. His four children, Michael, Patrick, John and Mary emigrated there in the 1820s, the latter two moving on to the USA. Michael (1801-83) settled in St John's, where he established a lime and paint business, dying intestate in 1883. His brother Patrick, on the other hand, settled at Red Head Cove, married Mary Doyle and had a large family of seven boys and seven girls. Many of their numerous descendants are still in Newfoundland.[20]

It has also been suggested that John the "Rapparee" may have been a brother of Robert Rice of Westcourt.[21] While it is possible that he was at least a distant blood relation, apart from being related by marriage to Jane Murphy, there are, however, grave difficulties in accepting that Robert and John were brothers. In the first place, if John were a brother of Robert, he would be married to his brother's step-daughter. This would, at the time have required a dispensation since the relationship was within the forbidden degrees of affinity. Then there was the age difference: John, as a brother of Robert, would be much older than Jane Murphy. He would, in fact, if he were Robert's brother, be even rather old for involvement in the United Irishmen.

Since his reputed brother, Robert, probably older, was born in the 1720s, John the "Rapparee" is unlikely to have been born later than 1735. The United Irish Club was founded by Wolf Tone in Belfast in 1791 and did not become a subversive group until 1793 when repressive legislation forced the leaders to abandon hope of bringing about parliamentary reform and getting religious grievances removed. Once negotiations for help from France were initiated the houses of the members were targeted for raids. This means that John Rice of Newlands would be about fifty eight years of age in 1793 when the raids began on the homes of members of the United Irishmen. Given the life expectancy of the time he would definitely be regarded as well beyond the age of fighting, though perhaps not of plotting. Like all nationalist movements, the United Irishmen attracted young men: Wolf Tone himself was not born until 1763 and even John Rice(born 1756) of New Ross was seven years older than Tone. It would, therefore, be surprising to have a man of his father's age active in the movement.

But this story poses an even greater problem: the difficulty of reconciling the political conservatism of the Callan Rices

Mount Trenchard, Foynes, Co. Limerick
Home of Spring Rice family

Portrait of
Thomas Spring Rice
while member for
Limerick (1820-32),
in studious pose.

with membership of and activity in such a radically subversive movement as Wolf Tone's United Irishmen. We can, therefore, only say that, while it is possible that "The Wild Rapparee" was actually the father of John Rice of New Ross, it is difficult to accept him as a son of grandfather Edmund, who was tax applotter of Callan in 1754, and brother of the stolid Robert of Westcourt.

Possible Limerick Connection
Some researchers make mention of a family tradition of a connection with Limerick Rices. This family tradition has been stated as follows: two Rice brothers had large estates in Limerick. One, named Thomas, became a Protestant circa 1708, in order to keep the estates. The other brother remained Catholic and moved to Callan and from Callan to New Ross.[22] Another family tradition states that three Rice brothers from Kerry came to settle in Kilkenny.[23]

In examining the possibility of a Limerick connection the first thing to note is that the more prominent Rices in Limerick are of Kerry origin. One of the better known is Thomas Spring-Rice (1790-1866), First Baron Monteagle, whose statue stands in the People's Square, Limerick. But more about this branch of the family later. First, let us look at some of the Kerry Rices.

One of the earliest of the Kerry Rices was Edward Rice of Dingle L'Couch, Dingle, Co. Kerry, of whom we have records dating from the time of Henry VIII. He married Anne Wall of County Limerick and had a son, Robert Rice. This Robert Rice married Juliana, daughter of Sir James Whyte Knt, of Cashel, Co. Tipperary. Among their children was Stephen Rice (d. 1623) of Dingle, Co. Kerry, who became MP for Kerry in 1613. He married Helen, daughter of Thomas Trant of Cahir Trant, Co. Kerry, and had two sons.[24]

The first of Stephen Rice's sons was James, who was MP for Dingle 1635. From him was descended Thomas Spring Rice MP of Mount Trenchard, Co. Limerick, who, as we noted above, was created first Baron Monteagle in 1839. The second son, Dominick, was also MP for Dingle in 1635 and married Alice, daughter of James Hussey, Baron of Galtrim, from which marriage descended Sir Stephen Rice, Knight, of Mount Rice, Lord Baron of the Court of the Exchequer in Ireland 1686.[25]

Lineage of the Spring-Rices

Stephen Edward Rice, of Mount Trenchard, Co. Limerick, son of Thomas Rice, and Mary, daughter of Maurice Fitzgerald, Knight of Glin, married, on 10 August 1785, Catherine, only child and heiress of Thomas Spring, of Castlemain, Kerry, and died 1831, leaving two daughters, Catherine Ann, who died unmarried, and Mary, who married Sir Aubrey De Vere, of Currachase, Co Limerick, and a son, Thomas Spring Rice, born 1790. The latter married Lady Theodosia Pery, daughter of the first Earl of Limerick. Among his children were Stephen Edmond, Thomas, who succeeded his father as Second Baron Monteagle, and Francis the fourth Baron.[26]

Just as the founder, Edmund, was the most prominent of the Callan Rices, so Thomas Spring Rice was the most prominent of the Limerick Rices. Born at Mount Trenchard, Foynes, near the south bank of the Shannon, Thomas was a member of the House of Commons from 1820 to his elevation to the Peerage as Baron Monteagle of Brandon in 1839. He represented Limerick City from 1820 to 1832 and Cambridge from 1832 to 1839. He was a cabinet minister in several Whig administrations holding the posts of Secretary of State for War and the Colonies, and Chancellor of the Exchequer. His name is well known in British Colonial history since it was he, as Secretary of State for the Colonies, who sent out the circular in 1833 intimating the intention of the British Government to introduce legislation to emancipate all slaves in the British possessions.[27]

The first Baron Monteagle was a man of great intellectual ability allied to a commitment to public affairs, especially the improvement of social and economic conditions in his own county and country. The citizens of Limerick showed their appreciation of his contribution on their behalf by erecting a monument to him in the People's Park. The people of Foynes also erected a memorial to his son, Stephen Spring Rice, in grateful appreciation of his efforts to improve the lot of his tenants.[28]

A great grand-daughter of the first Baron Monteagle with nationalist tendencies, Mary Spring Rice, first concocted the plan of importing arms from Germany for the "volunteers", using an old trading smack based at Foynes. Her friend, Erskine Childers, agreed to help, but insisted on using his own yacht, the *Asgard*, with Mary crewing for him. Mary's cousin, Conor O'Brien, from

Brother Michael Mark Hill 1847-1919

Foynes, skippered the other vessel, the *Kelpie*, crewed by his sister, Kitty and two men from Foynes. It is not well known that it was the donations of Mary Spring Rice's friends, all members of the Limerick gentry, which paid for the German rifles imported in these two boats.[29]

My own family has a slight connection with the Spring-Rices in that my uncle, Michael Feheney (1860-1939), opposed the second Baron Monteagle (1849-1926) in the first Irish Local Government elections of 1899 for the Askeaton seat in the Limerick County Council. This was the 'pre-Sinn Féin' period and my uncle's nationalism was that of John Redmond's Home Rule Party, while the Baron was listed as a Unionist. When the votes were counted it was found that the Baron had defeated my uncle by some two hundred votes. However, my uncle lodged an appeal on some technical grounds and the Baron's election was declared unconstitutional, my uncle taking the seat in his place. The Baron declined to contest subsequent elections, held every three years, so my uncle retained possession of the seat until he retired.[30]

As the family history of the Mount Trenchard Rices is well documented since the 1700s, and there is no mention in it of a connection with the Callan Rices, it is highly unlikely that such a connection exists.[31]

Sir Stephen Rice
Another suggestion of a possible connection between the Callan and Limerick Rices is through Sir Stephen Rice, Chancellor of the Exchequer in Ireland in 1687 under James II. Following the defeat of James's army at the Boyne and Aughrim in 1690, and the Treaty of Limerick in 1691, Sir Stephen, in common with other Jacobins, lost his post, but unlike them, was allowed, most probably in return for some form of collaboration with the new Williamite administration, to retain possession of his personal property. Lenihan's *History of Limerick*, has been quoted in connection with one of Sir Stephen's sons "conformed" to the Protestant religion to inherit his father's property while the other son was "informed against". It has been suggested that this particular son may then have left Limerick for Callan.[32]

This theory does not, however, hold up under closer scrutiny. The Founder's Rices were well established in Callan long before

Sir Stephen's death in 1714. The Founder's granduncle, Patrick Rice, of Attatinoe, made a will in 1771 at the age of eighty five. This means that he was born in 1686, when Sir Stephen was in his prime and about to become Chancellor of the Irish Exhequer. Moreover, Patrick mentions two other brothers, Edmund, the Founder's grandfather, and Thomas, in addition to a sister, Margaret, in his will, as well as other Rices, who appear to be relatives, all living in the area.[33] There is no suggestion that they had lately come to live in the area. Information from other sources also suggests that the Rices of Callan were in the locality, including the townlands of Cuffesgrange, Tullamaine, Attatinoe and Westcourt, and had been there for several generations.[34] An examination of the dates does not even permit us to entertain the possibility that they were descended from Sir Stephen Rice's son who remained a Catholic.

A Limerick Connection Still Possible
Though we have to dismiss the suggestions that a connection between the Limerick and Callan Rices came about through either Sir Stephen Rice or the Spring Rices, we do not have to dismiss outright either the idea that the Callan Rices originally came from Limerick or that they had some connection with Sir Stephen Rice. The late Brother Loyola Rice (descended from the Founder's nephew, Patrick, who emigrated to Newfoundland, and who was a dedicated collector of Rice family traditions), refers to Sir Stephen helping a relative, Patrick Rice, acquire some property there.[35] These little anecdotes and morsels of information emphasise the fact that a genealogist must never discount a family tradition. There is usually a truth behind it, though the real connection may differ from the reported one. Each story teller inevitably adds his/her own creativity to the story. We can only conclude, therefore, that much more research needs to be done on the family history of the Callan Rices before we can substantiate a claim of a Limerick connection.

We can, however, say that the Callan Rices were "well-connected", enterprising, sober, and industrious with an eye for a good business deal. Moreover, they enjoyed the confidence and trust, if not the patronage, of the local landlords and Establishment and generally avoided involvement in nationalist movements.

One of the most notable things about the Callan Rices is their comparative wealth in a period when even Catholic members of the native aristocracy and landed gentry who remained in Ireland were reduced to poverty. At the height of the penal laws, in 1771, Patrick Rice of Attatinoe had a lease of one hundred acres of good land when the average holding of an Irish Catholic was five to ten acres. Moreover, in his will he expressly disposes of a sum of money, which, today, would be the equivalent of not less than £150,000.[36] The Founder's father, Robert Rice, at the same time, had a lease of one hundred and eighty acres. Such leases were not granted to peasant Catholics. The Rices had to have important connections.

Similarly, the respect in which the Founder was held was unlikely to be due solely to his own ability and personality, even when allied to wealth and great personal probity. His family also had to have social status. And none were better than the Irish at reading the unspoken language of class and social status.[37] There is good reason to suggest that the good "Mr. Rice" was welcome in the houses of the powerful and wealthy firstly because he belonged to the middle class and his family was an old and respected one and only secondly because of his wealth and personal qualities.

The Norman Rices
Before I conclude it may be helpful to put the questions discussed above within the context of the overall history of the Rhys/Rice family over the past several hundred years. The following paragraphs constitute no more than a thumbnail sketch, highlighting some of the achievements of a family that has, hitherto, received little attention from family historians.

The Rices of Leinster and Munster are of Welsh origin, the original name being Ruys, Rys and Rhys. The family came to England with William the Conqueror in 1066 and settled in Wales. One of them, Rys of Towdave Maur, is said to have been the last independent Prince of Wales. His daughter Nesta was known as the "Helen of Wales" and her descendants the Rhys, FitzGeralds, FitzStephens and Barrys came to Ireland with the Norman invasion in the twelfth century. Though the Rhys settled in Wexford, Waterford, Limerick and Kerry, there is a curious connection with the city of Galway, for the pilot traditionally believed to have accompanied Christopher Columbus on his voyage of discovery, and even to have sailed to America on his own, was Rice de Galvey.[38]

From the early fourteenth century onwards the Rices (Rhys) feature in the public and civic life of these counties, holding appointments as provosts, mayors, and sheriffs. There was a Richard Rys in New Ross in 1305. The *Red Book of Ormond* records the names of Philip, William, John and Matthew Rys, who occupied the manor of Knocktopher in 1312. The *Calendar of Ormond Deeds* records a "town land of Ricelands called from the family Rys or Rice." situated near Knocktopher. James Rice was Mayor of Waterford in 1423. In 1294 John Rice was Lord Treasurer of Ireland. Walter Rice was Mayor of Limerick 1520. Robert Rice was Bishop of Ferns in 1666-67. Edward Rice represented Askeaton, Co. Limerick, in the "Patriot Parliament" of 1689, when the country was rallying behind James II. James Louis, Count Rice's house in Dingle was prepared as a refuge for Marie Antoinette during the French Revolution as part of the ill-fated rescue plan that never got going. The Count was an officer in the Austrian army and friend of Emperor Joseph II, as well as being a famous duellist.[39]

This article is being written in a period of transition in Irish genealogy when parish records, our main source of recorded genealogical information, are being computerised. This computerisation is being undertaken under the auspices of the Irish Genealogical Project (IGP). On successful completion of this project it will not only be possible to consult records in each area/diocese but to access a general index through a "signposting" system available through a central computer with terminals at civic and tourist centres. When this period comes it will be much easier to trace the different members of the Rice diaspora.

Meantime we can only encourage and affirm those enthusiasts who are now prepared to do the inevitable "leg work" associated with family history research. Let us never forget, however, that much invaluable work can be done by collecting oral information and traditions handed down within the family. Some of our youngest Rice researchers have given an excellent demonstration of this recently.[40]

Aspects of Rice Family History

References

1 I would like to acknowledge the help and advice of several people in preparing this article for publication: Joe Rice in Australia for arousing my curiosity in Rice genealogy, Bride Roe, New Ross, for information, advice and enthusiasm, James Rice, Ballinhassig, Co. Cork, for information on his branch of the family, Miriam Kelly for permission to draw from her research into her branch of the Rice family, Br. Brendan Kelleher for information, Brs. Frank Keane CFC and Justinian Collins FPM for reading an early draft of this article and making suggestions.

2 Joe got my name and telephone number from his brother-in-law, John O'Shaughnessy, also living in Victoria, whom I had helped in his research leading to the construction of a family tree.

3 County and City of Cork Postal Directory, 1844.

4 Baptism and Marriage Register of Church of Ss Peter & Paul, Cork

5 R. H. Laing, Cork Mercantile Directory, 1863

6 Henry and Coghlan, Directory of Cork and Munster, 1867, p. 143

7 James Rice, Ballyhooley Road, Cork, to J. M. Feheney, private conversation, August 1990.

8 James Rice, Ballyhooley Road, Cork, to J. M. Feheney, private conversation, August 1990.

9 Richard Griffith, Primary Valuation of Lands and Tenements, 1850, Ballinaboy parish, Union of Cork & Kinsale.

10 See family tree, "FT01:Rice Family of Callan".

11 Baptismal Register, Ballybricken Parish, Waterford.

12 Joe Rice to J. M. Feheney, private correspondence 23 October, 1990

13 John Mannion of Memorial University of Newfoundland notes that Edmund Rice was listed as either a victualler or a gentleman but not as a "merchant". In 1799 he is recorded as having an interest in a tavern (The Garter Inn) in Callan, which may be the one operated by his brother, Thomas, recorded as a publican in Callan in 1787. John Mannion to Bride Roe, private correspondence 2 Jan, 1992.

14 See Family Tree chart, "FT03:Rice Family of New Ross", drawn by J. M. Feheney 1993 from original prepared by Bride Roe 1984.

15 James Warren Doyle, born New Ross 1786, witnessed battle 1798, ordained 1809, bishop of Kildare and Leighlin 1819 (hence initials "JKL"), died Carlow 1834. Was first Irish prelate to join Catholic Association.

16 See accompanying "FT 03:Rice Family of New Ross".

17 Bride Roe to J. M. Feheney, private communication, 13 Dec 1993.

18 M. C. Normoyle, A Tree is Planted (Christian Brothers, Dublin, 2nd ed 1976), p. 82; also Bride Roe's family tree chart of New Ross Rices 1984.

19 Brother F. R. Foran, Edmund Rice Centre, Freshwater, Newfoundland, private correspondence to Bride Roe, 8 Dec 1988.

20 See accompanying family tree, "FT02:Rice Family of Newfoundland", information for which was kindly provided by Bride Roe, New Ross.

21 See accompanying Family Tree chart, "FT03:Rice Family of New Ross". An information leaflet, "The Rice Family in Newfoundland" from the Edmund Rice Information Center, St John, Newfoundland, kindly supplied by Bride Roe, suggests that the "Wild Rapparee" was neither a relative of the Founder nor a Catholic.

22 Bride Roe to J. M. Feheney, private correspondence, 20 March 1991 and Rice Family Tree by Miriam Kelly and Elizabeth Manning on display at the Edmund Rice Centre, Callan. Kilkenny Standard Monthly Review of September 1989 is well ahead of present research when it states that "Edmund Rice's grandfather was Lord Monteagle of Limerick. The title was not, however, continued by Lord Monteagle's oldest son, Catholic Robert Rice, father of Edmund".

23 Bride Roe to J. M. Feheney, private communication, 13 Dec 1993. Bride got this information from Michael Rice, a farmer, of Burnchurch, Co. Kilkenny. This Michael Rice was a descendant of the Founder's uncle, Maurice Rice, who owned the Clubhouse Hotel in Kilkenny.

24 Burke's *Landed Gentry of Ireland* (London, 1912), "Rice of Bushmount", pp. 388-9.

25 Ibid.

26 Burke, *Peerage, Baronetage and Knightage* (104th ed, London 1967), p. 1747.

27 Ibid.

28 David Fitzpatrick, "Thomas Spring Rice and the Peopling of Australia", The *Old Limerick Journal*, Number 23, Spring 1988, pp. 39-49.

29 Ibid. Conor O'Brien was the father of Conor Cruise O'Brien, the well-known author and journalist.

30 Colman Moloney, "Limerick County Council 1899-1932", MA Thesis, UCC, 1977, appendix.

31 Burke, *Peerage, Baronetage and Knightage* (London, 1967), p. 1747.

32 Bride Roe to J. M. Feheney, private correspondence, 20 March, 1991.

33 Last Will and Testament of Patrick Rice, Attatinoe, 21 February, 1771.

34 M. C. Normoyle, op. cit., p. 1.

35 I am indebted to Bride Roe for this reference.

36 Last Will and Testament of Patrick Rice, Attatinoe, 21 February, 1771.

37 John Waters, *Jiving at the Crossroads* (Blackstaff Press, 1991), pp. 31-33.

38 Edward MacLysaght, *Irish Families: Their Names, Arms and Origins* (3rd ed 1972), p. 143.

39 Ibid.

40 See Rice Family Tree on display in Edmund Rice Centre, Callan. This was compiled by Miriam Kelly and Elizabeth Manning and is the source used in drawing our family tree diagram, "FT01:Rice Family of Callan".

The Death of Mrs. Edmund Rice

Liam P. Ó Caithnia, CFC

N OT ONLY DO WE not know with any degree of certainty the Christian name or the surname of the wife of Edmund Rice[1] but we do not as yet know her age,[2] her religious persuasion,[3] her place of birth[4] or her occupation – if she had one. We have however two separate, distinct and, so far as I know, unrelated accounts of her untimely death. The first of these was written by Sister Josephine Rice, Mercy Convent, Belvedere, St. John's, Newfoundland and will be found in *A Tree is Planted*, p. 25. where it was published verbatim as it was given by her to Br. J. G. Hogan, Assistant to the Superior General of the Christian Brothers, in 1930:

> The Founder had been married to a lady of a well-to-do family[5] who was fond of the hunt as most wealthy people[6] were in those days. When she was well-advanced with child, she went riding and was thrown from her horse, dying as a result of the accident. The doctor managed to save the child who had evidently been injured by the fall and hence did not develop normally.[7] This was the child he provided for when he began his work.[8]

I trust an observant reader will be forgiven for wondering whether this is in fact the account written by Sr. Josephine or is it perhaps Gregory Hogan's version of what Sr. Josephine said? Lest it appear ill-mannered to question it we must remember that all such statements are made with intent to assure the reader of the truth, detailed and absolute, of what is asserted in them and I do not feel totally assured that Gregory Hogan's report, as I find it here, is in keeping with such standards. Moreover it is scarcely possible that Br. Hogan could have had any experience of the principles and methodology of professional collectors. I suggest this in all good faith and salute the man for his most important contribution. One must wonder however would Sister Josephine have referred to Edmund Rice as 'the Founder' in 1930 – or is the nomenclature Gregory Hogan's? Would we, in talking to a Presentation Sister, speak of Nano Nagle or the 'Foundress'? In talking to a Mercy Sister would we say 'Catherine McAuley' or the 'Foundress'? Without stressing the matter unduly, I suggest the difference here is between internal and external writing. Founder/Foundress is ordinarily used *within* an Institute. If, on foot of folklore or tradition within her own family in Newfoundland, Sister Josephiné knew so much of the family whose daughter was Edmund Rice's wife, is it not most extraordinary that she did not mention the surname of that family, their place of residence or their religious persuasion, nor did she profess ever to have been in possession of such information for, after all, forgetfulness is part of our human heritage. This is all the more remarkable if, at a time of universal misery and poverty, the young bride was "a lady of a well-to-do family who was fond of the hunt". Note too that Sister does not seem to have known that Mrs. Rice was most likely to have been married at 15 or 16 as virtually all Irish girls were, *regardless of* class. Would she, at that age, have been *accustomed* to hunt? Such an impression is not given by Dorothea Herbert! I confess that I am unsure but I doubt Edmund Rice's young wife would have done so, more especially if she were "well-advanced with child," and I harbour a gnawing doubt that Sister would have believed it either had she known the age of marriageable girls at that time.

One hesitates to press too far the case for a closer examination of Sister Josephine's contribution but it is fair to note the extraordinary lack of *any detail of concrete information* throughout. The more frequently one reads the account of the riding accident and the more familiar one gets with recorded tradition, genuine and spurious, the more suspect becomes the story of the fall, not particularly for what it says, though that too is suspect, but for what it leaves unsaid. The young lady is not named, she is not surnamed nor is any suggestion made touching her family except to remark that they were well-to-do. There is a strangeness too about the suggestion that the unborn "baby had *evidently* been injured by the fall," as though they were not quite sure – and not without reason! We shall have occasion to touch on that again. I skip a number of other factors (referring to a 15 or 16-year old girl as a lady! and offering no clue whatever as to the identity of the doctor) but respectfully request the reader to check once more the last sentence in the extract cited above and attributed to Sr. Josephine. "This was the child he provided for when he began his work." I find the curt singular pronoun – '*he* provided . . . *he* began' strangely jarring, as I do the reference to '*his* work'. Is it the comment of Sister Josephine at all or is it a Gregory Hogan give-away gloss? How could *she* have known in 1929 that '*he*' had made provision for the child since, as Br. Colm Normoyle reminds us "*she* (the child) was not even *mentioned* in the early biographies of the Founder", nor, I may add, in the early biographical sketches of Father Fitzgerald,[9] Maurice Lenihan,[10] John Austin Grace,[11] Tom Hearne,[12] Pat Corbett[13] or anyone else that I know of. One hopes to be pardoned for doubting seriously that the story of the fall from a horse should have been so well remembered in Newfoundland – from 1789 to 1929 – 140 years! – or even known at all, and so thoroughly 'disremembered' all over Ireland![14]

It is no less perplexing to find that the Newfoundland Rices knew how Edmund's wife died – if they did know? – but had forgotten both her name and her surname! It challenges belief indeed to be told that throughout all of that time both the name and surname of Edmund Rice's young, deceased wife were forgotten wholly, whether by accident or design! They are unknown to this day.[15] Is it not asking too much of us to accept that the sad story of her death was well remembered by a family of the Rices in Newfoundland but not, apparently, by *any* of the Rices of Callan, Waterford, New Ross or anywhere else? None of the Callan neighbours appear to have heard of it, which is strange since Tom Heron was of the opinion "that the Rices were connected in many ways with Callan families".[16] Nor are we dependent on Tom Heron alone for such an assurance: Fr. Patrick O'Brien, O.S.A., who was Prior of the Augustinians of Callan for at least nine terms (between 1883 and 1919) and was related by marriage to relatives of Edmund Rice, assures us that Edmund "was related to all the independent farmers in this (Callan) locality".[17] Nevertheless, nobody knew the story of the fall from the horse – if there was a fall?

There is not a glimmer of memory related to horse-riding in *Memories* itself, a book saturated with recollections of Edmund Rice, in Waterford as well as in Callan. Moreover the memory of Edmund's wife was recalled clearly in Callan: "Most of the old people here (Callan) knew that Edmund Rice was married"[18] although her name had been forgotten. Tom Heron confessed "I heard the name of Edmund Rice's wife also but I fail to recall it".[19] There is not therefore, prior to 1929, or since then, any echo of such an accident having been recorded in Waterford or in Callan or associated anywhere with Mrs. Rice apart from one solitary witness. Are we justified therefore in referring to it as the "Rice family tradition"[20] when in fact there is not a scintilla of evidence of such a tradition having been known to any member of any branch of the Rice family anywhere in Ireland – even in Newfoundland?

One is aware, of course, of the danger of the *argumentum ex silentio* – 'nobody ever heard of it so it cannot be true!' – but when the silence is so absolute and so sustained one must be excused for seeking some positive evidence to justify unbroken faith in a localised claim so flimsily accredited. Is it not remarkable that, of "no fewer than 250 witnesses" whose testimony is, with due solemnity, recorded in *Memories*[21] not even one indicated familiarity with such a tragedy? Not only so, but in 376 pages of precisely such memories only one person, an eighty-year-old man, ventured to give her a name and a surname, when asked to do so, whilst acknowledging that he was unsure of both![22] And that was 160 years after her death!

Whether we like it or not, we shall have to take an uncompromising stand in deciding on the hard facts that are so necessary if we are to carry Edmund Rice's biography a step beyond the excellence of *A Tree Is Planted*. Ordinarily, professionally trained collectors of folklore affix an agreed printed questionnaire to the statement, account, incident, evidence, or whatever has been dictated by the responsible informant. Some of the questions to which answers are normally requested in such an investigation are these: (i) name of informant before and after marriage, (ii) place of birth, early life and later life, (iii) present address (townland, parish, barony and county), (iii) approximate age, (iv) religious persuasion, if any, (v) source(s) of information, that is, name of informant's own immediate informant and probable antecedent sources known to these, (vi) name of collector, (vii) place and date of transcription. In this way one can be reasonably assured that what the informant stated is word-accurate and may be received with a reasonable degree of conviction. Moreover the nature of the informant's background can often be assessed: the likelihood of such information having survived in a given time and place and having been accurately retained by the informant, and so on.

The Death of Mrs. Edmund Rice

Professional collectors are quick to note and assess such pointers. The *caveat* of Carl Von Sydow is worth noting:

> just as the historian must weigh the trustworthiness, kind, age, and origin of the sources, so must the student of popular tradition.

Suffice here, for the moment, to pause and note that none of these necessary, well-established specifics accompany the statement attributed to Sister Josephine. For that very reason alone, and regardless of whatever merit may attach to it, it is wanting in the professional finesse that might otherwise have buttressed the evidence it adduces. Hence our muted doubt!

What therefore can the origin of the motif of 'the fall from the horse' be, assuming Mrs. Rice did indeed fall from a horse – if it is not what it purports to be: the occasion of her death? I, for my part, do not think it was that. Before presuming to consider a plausible explanation for it, or any explanation at all, perhaps we would be well advised first of all to examine an alternative, though less well-publicised, account of the death of Mrs. Rice. So far as I know nobody had suggested a reason for her death other than the fall from the horse until John Power, 38 O'Connell Street, Waterford, was interviewed by Br. W. B. Cullen in July 1949, twenty years later than Gregory Hogan's interview with Sr. Josephine and 160 years after the event it purports to explain. The portion of John Power's contribution which is of significance for us is as follows:

> I heard my father say that Edmund Rice's wife is buried in an old graveyard near the site of the present Court House, Waterford, which was then outside the city walls. There was fever in the city and it was thought she contracted the fever and died. All my family had great veneration for Br. Rice . . . My father prided himself on his knowledge of Br. Rice's affairs. I distinctly recollect his statement relative to the death of Edmund Rice's wife. Peter Power, my father, was a great local historian.[23]

It need scarcely be added that Br. W. B. Cullen bore sworn witness before a Commissioner of Oaths to the accuracy of this transcription of the contribution of John F. Power which is of

71

such importance to us today. Since my purpose is to compare and contrast the two surviving traditions touching the death of Mrs. Rice we may concede straight away that the Waterford tradition – for such it is, as distinct from folklore – seems to be the likelier of the two: it is a unique tradition in the sense that it has no variants known to us and we feel assured that the informant, known antecedents, and collector are dependably trustworthy.

We are in no doubt what that tradition was, for John Power recalled it in a solemn statement that was duly copied, verbatim, and sworn to by Br. Cullen. We have no such *published* sworn assurance of the objective and absolute accuracy of the story recalled by Sister Josephine. If we adhere to what has been published in *A Tree* then we may even doubt that it is her own transcription at all, however trustworthy it may be as a précis of what Sister said. Moreover, one must unfortunately acknowledge that while she has laid us all under her contribution she has given us no satisfactory reason to accept a story which is at best a single dubious link in a chain of evidence that, if we are to judge by the statement attributed to her, was known only to herself. John Power's evidence is impressively brief, clear, subdued and specific. We know who his immediate informant was, we are aware of that informant's abiding interest in Edmund Rice's apostolate and we can believe and accept that the tradition he had inherited is quite likely to extend unbroken back to the mid-19th century if not earlier. One notes also the caution implicit in his evidence: "it was *thought* she contracted *the* fever" – clearly, a specific fever – but he entertained no such doubt touching the memory of his father who "prided himself on his knowledge of Br. Rice's affairs" for he "was a great (amateur) historian." Nevertheless the evidence briefly halts, for all unique traditions need to be accountable in an unbroken line of descent from sure source to dependable record and John Power cannot claim a source as early as 1789. He redeems himself however by claiming that 160 years before he spoke a fever raged in Waterford, a fever in which he suggests Mrs. Rice may well have died. The researcher cannot neglect the obligation to seek for evidence of such a fever for if there was one in Waterford in 1789 it must add immense prestige to the claim of John Power.

None of those who contributed to *Memories* had borne witness to such a catastrophe in Waterford in the lifetime of Edmund

Rice, nor did the Powers trouble themselves to ensure the truth or probability of it or instance further evidence in its support. It was part of their tradition and no more. If such a fever had swept the land in 1789 would it not go a long way to justify us in accepting the contribution so well remembered in 1949 by the Powers of Waterford? Very little research was required to prove that such a fever did indeed sweep the land in that year and was the cause of death for many thousands in Ireland, rich and poor, and many millions overseas. It is moreover a strange coincidence that the memory of it – the only one I have seen – should be enshrined in the personal diary (1770-1806) of a most unhappy woman, Dorothea Herbert, whose uncle, Lord John Cuffe, was Robert Rice's landlord and a figure remembered, not without affection and some admiration, by the people of Callan. Lord Cuffe was a great follower of hurling and was called John o' the Cap because he wore his team colours with pride and he wore them in his expensive cap (as jockeys still do) but his cap was the envy of all!

In the year 1789, the year in which Mrs. Rice – probably but not certainly the wife of Edmund Rice – died, Dorothea Herbert wrote in her *Recollections* (1770-1806), late in May of that year:

> About this time a dreadful Fever raged all over the World (I may say) and carried off Millions in every quarter of the Globe – Scarce a family was there but felt its Effects – Mr. Hare lost his third son Robert, and Mrs. Cox of Castletown her fourth son William – both died in the West Indies – Mr. Wilson of Carrick our Attorney died of it in Dublin, and left a large family – in short the Victims within our small Acquaintance were too numerous to reckon.[24]

This does not exhaust the evidence of Miss Herbert however. Throughout the following year, 1790, the fever raged on and our diarist later recalled:

> My sister Sophy was seized with the same fever that carried off such numbers all over the world the preceding year. It was highly infectious and none of our friends would venture near the house. The servant boy took it and we were in hourly dread of it spreading through the family – however it went no further though Sophy was totally given over. I hardly ever saw anyone worse. She lay some weeks at the jaws of death and

her sufferings from a pain in her bones were dreadful. My Aunt Blunden fled at its first appearance and we were a long time shut up on quarantine. However both patients recovered.[25]

Was this fever the real cause of Mrs. Rice's death? I think so. Br. Colm Normoyle who appears not to have known of the Power tradition in 1976 (it is not mentioned in *A Tree*) felt indisposed to reject either tradition and, whilst editing *Memories*, suggested a compromise between the fever and the fall from a horse:

> the two traditions can easily be reconciled if it is assumed that because of the pregnancy and the fall a fever developed which proved fatal.[26]

One is tempted to ask whether it is an improvement on "she fell and died" to assume that "she fell and caught fever" – and then died? In any case it needs to be said that assumptions such as this have no respected place in the study of social history for nothing entitles us to assume that to be true for which there is no *evidence* and I do not believe that there is any satisfactory evidence, however likely it may be, that Mrs. Rice ever sat a horse, much less that she did so in late pregnancy and then fell off it. In any event there is no necessity to associate the fever with a fall from a horse when we know that such a fever already raged through Europe and beyond it.

It seems to me quite credible that if Mrs. Rice had died in hospital of a fever of such magnitude that "scarce a family was there but felt its effects," that her death might indeed have been forgotten in a cloud of national amnesia, unconsciously induced perhaps, given the awesome fear of fevers in those years. Moreover since Mrs. Rice may not have been more than seven or eight months married at the time of her death – we cannot (and ought not) guess how long – she was very likely to have been a little-known teenage girl, a solitary name in one of a long list of sad, daily and frightening obituaries. Neither of course would young Mr. Rice have been in 1789 the figure of consequence he became several decades later. His wife might well have died of a fever which claimed so many of the high and mighty and soon have been forgotten by all but the circle who had known and loved her.

How then account for the *motif* of the fall from a horse? For my

The Death of Mrs. Edmund Rice

part I do not believe that Edmund Rice's wife died as a result of a fall from any horse but that the motif of the fall can be accounted for and is correctly related, not to the mother but to the child. It is but one of several similar motifs commonly invoked in former times and continued to be so down to the last generation, in many parts of Ireland, and even to the present day, if only infrequently. Often, when a newly-born child was found to be delicate, to have a physical defect or an unaccountable birth-mark or a mental weakness of some description, the parents or grandparents would quietly remark that "of course" *their* family was never blemished in any such way but that the mother, during her pregnancy (a) fell off a horse, or (b) was kicked by a horse, or (c) fell down the stairs (an excellent indication that the family had a two-storeyed house when such were rare!) or (d) got a kick from a cow while milking, or (e) slipped while stepping down from a (pony and) trap – or whatever. Almost anything sufficed by way of explanation providing the good *name* of the family was not impugned.

Sometimes such a story took time to grow, more especially if the problem of the child were a mental one, for that might not become apparent until the infant was some few years old. If, then, Mary Rice were found to have been 'delicate' (a word found several times in *Memories*) upon her arrival in Callan, nothing was more likely than that the kindly people of Westcourt would accomodate the sensitivity of the Rices by assuring all concerned that the girl's mother had, *no doubt*, fallen from a horse! Perhaps Michael Rice, Edmund's brother, believed it: he seems undoubtedly to have passed it on to his family before or after he had reached St. John's, Newfoundland. Sr. Josephine, his grand-daughter, clearly believed it and has borne testimony to that fact. It is however dubious in its origin, unsatisfactory in the methodology of its recording and open to very serious doubt in its descent. Fall or fever, therefore, the choice is ours!

References

1 Both the christian name, Mary, and the surname, Elliott, given her in modern biographies of Edmund Rice were suggested by Martin O'Flynn *160* years after her death. No name was given her throughout these years so far as I know. Mr. O'Flynn confessed with commendable honesty that he was in doubt concerning both the christian name Mary (it was 'Bridget or Mary', he said) and the surname, Elliott ("if I don't mistake", he added). So many questions are begged here that, with no disrespect to the memory of Mr. O'Flynn, I have thought it wise to exclude Mrs.

A Man Raised Up

Rice's name altogether from this brief essay. An added vexation for the researcher is the fact that the building used by Br. Rice for his first classes in New Street was known as Elliotts! It should be said in favour of Mr. O'Flynn's contribution however that Elliott is a name frequently met with in Waterford and is commonly interchanged with Ellis, Elligot and other similar forms. Moreover it is but fair to note that Mr.O'Flynn's grandfather was a first cousin of Edmund Rice. For all that I am not satisfied that the evidence for 'Elliott' is satisfactory.

2 Almost all females, rich and poor, were married at 15 or 16 at that time – sometimes younger! So common was this that one would need very sure and specific evidence if one were to suggest that Mrs. Rice was at all older.

3 Mrs. Edmund Rice need not have been a Roman Catholic. There are no sufficient reasons for believing that she was. Mixed marriages were common in the second half of the 18th century.

4 Nothing is known of this. It is assumed, without evidence, to have been Waterford.

5 Mrs. Rice was *140 years dead* when this tradition was first revealed in Newfoundland in 1929. It is surely remarkable that such a story never appears to have been known to the Rices or was not acknowledged by them if they knew of it. This includes the Rices of Callan, Waterford and New Ross. Neither do any of the Elliotts appear to have heard of it – or of Edmund Rice for that matter. No bond is known to have been forged between the Elliotts and the Rices before or after 1789. Moreover, if young Mrs. Rice's family were so well off and lived in Waterford, or nearby, why did they not take her baby daughter after the death of its mother – whether by fall or by fever? If they wished to take her and Edmund Rice refused to grant them this reasonable request, why did he do so?

6 Dorothea Herbert, a niece of the Rices' landlord, Lord John Cuffe, never once suggested that she or any of her coevals engaged in hunting. She was about Edmund Rice's age. Two of her closest girl-friends married at the age of "fifteen or sixteen." Most readers would need concrete evidence that pregnant young wives (15 to18 years, say) followed the hunt before they would *assume* that Mrs. Rice did so.

7 Nothing is known with certainty of Mary Rice that suggests she was either abnormal or handicapped, as these words are understood nowadays. She was 'delicate' as was her *cousin*, young Richard Rice, to whom the same word, 'delicate', was applied, yet nobody ever suggests *he* was abnormal or handicapped mentally or physically. I have sought in vain for a meaning indicative of abnormality in the use of the word 'delicate' in all the Rice literature, printed and manuscript. The Callan folk who recalled memories of Mary Rice (Edmund's daughter), in the forties of the *present* century, at no time suggested she was handicapped or that she "had evidently been injured by the fall and hence did not develop normally," as Sr. Josephine recalled. It is to be noted therefore that whatever illness, if any, made an exception of the girl is, in Sister Josephine's account, expressly related ('*hence*') to the Newfoundland tradition of the fall from the horse – a fall that never was? Some Callan folk who had seen and met her had understood that she had entered a convent. See *A Tree* p. 27

8 "Mary Rice was maintained in comfort by the Congregation until her death in January 1859." See *A Tree* p. 311.

9 Rev. Fr. Richard Fitzgerald, who had been confessor to the Brothers in Mount Sion for many years, was Administrator in the Cathedral from 1843 to 1862 and gave the sermon at the Month's Mind for Edmund Rice, 1 October 1844. The sermon ran to close on 10,500 words and will be found in *Memories*, No. 68 [pp 97-109]

10 Maurice Lenihan (whose *History of Limerick* is often referred to merely as Lenihan) wrote c. 2750 words on the death of Edmund Rice in the *Tipperary Vindicator*, a newspaper founded and edited by Lenihan himself. No other notice, in any newspaper, could compare with Lenihan's contribution. It is reproduced in *Memories* No. 251 [pp 331-337]. See next note.

The Death of Mrs. Edmund Rice

11 Br. John A. Grace is believed to have written the article on Edmund Rice which appeared in the Biographical Register shortly after his death. It was the longest of all the tributes to Edmund Rice. It is No. 263 in *Memories*, pp. 348-357. John A. Grace was a native of Capaheadon and a neighbour of the Rices of Westcourt, Callan. Br. Normoyle felt that Brother Grace drew freely on Lenihan's account in the *Tipperary Vindicator*. See n.11

12 Br. Tom Hearne, who knew Br. Rice well and worked with him has left us a brief account, useful and provocative, of his life and accomplishments: c.2,500 words.

13 Br. Patrick Corbett, who spent many years in Carrick-on-Suir knew Br. Rice better than most and left a short account of his life. Like Br. J. A. Grace, he was inaccurate in some details.

14 I am not aware that anybody who was related in any way to the Rices or the Elliotts had ever suggested that the Rices hunted nor was there ever an echo, however faint, of the tradition of a fall from a horse until Sr. Josephine made it known in Canada in 1929.

15 It is surely remarkable that not only did the Rices forget the name of Edmund's wife in a small city where Edmund was, and continued to be, particularly well-known, but that the Elliotts (or whoever Edmund's in-laws were) also appear to have forgotten it or deliberately chose to forget it. If one were to assume however that Mrs. Rice was not a Catholic – and at the end of the 18th Century mixed marriages were commonplace – then her demise at the time of young Mary's birth could have occasioned a bitter and permanent breach between Edmund and his in-laws. That is not unlikely because, by a traditional matrimonial arrangement, the girls assumed the religious beliefs of the mother and the boys those of the father. Edmund Rice would not have been blind to the implications of this tradition (which still holds good in many places), hence a serious crisis may well have arisen between the Rices and Elliotts touching the religious persuasion in which the baby girl was to be baptised. This might account for the immediacy of Joan Rice's call to Waterford and the removal of young Mary at a later time from thence to Callan. Much closer research will be required however to challenge and establish all the probabilities and possibilities of this theory. How likely is it, for example, that a Protestant girl – any Protestant girl – would have been called Mary (Elliott)? On the other hand, if Edmund did choose to marry outside the church of his own family, might that not explain the strange comment of Maurice Lenihan to which the attention of the reader is drawn in note 47 of the essay *Edmund Rice and His Social Milieu*?

16 *Memories* p. 137

17 *Memories* p. 218.

18 *Memories* p. 142

19 *Memories* p. 138

20 It is so referred to in *Memories* No 179 (p. 242, footnote 2).

21 249 submissions were made by named witnesses, 21 are taken from published reports. One is tempted to ask here how the early Brothers can have forgotten *everything* about the married life of their Founder, particularly the name of his wife. Some of them, after all, like Br. Kieran Flynn, were related to him. Others, like J. A. Grace, were neighbours' children. (Br. Grace's uncle had taught the young Rices.) Can they all have forgotten overnight? And why have the Eliotts never *claimed* the honour of having had Edmund Rice – Waterford's *greatest son*! – as a son-in-law? It is, of course, possible that the Elliotts were not a Waterford family and that the brevity of their relationship with the Rices might suffice in itself to explain the forgetfulness but this argument is not convincing. If the breach on the other hand was one of conspiracy, as it may well have been, what caused it? Two factors occur to me by way of explanation (i) the Rices were never easy communicators – they themselves realised that and, more specifically, (ii) Edmund Rice scarcely ever referred to himself

at all! Having spoken with the greatest respect for this many-branched family, Thomas Heron, who knew them so well, concluded: "There was an element of aloofness about them all." Br. Pat Corbett, who knew Edmund so well, got his father's name wrong and Br. J. A. Grace got the number of his brothers wrong – a reasonable indication of how little they exchanged family news! Br. M. L. Rice of Cuffesgrange (5 miles from Callan) said to me once, "all the Rices are the same – they can't talk." Small wonder that Austin Dunphy, the Christian Brother who, of all others, was most likely to have known Edmund Rice best, was impelled to confess to John Austin Grace after the great man's death "very little can now be known of his early life" (*Memories* p. 88), an indication, surely, that Edmund Rice was not a memorable communicator!

22 *Memories* p. 224
23 *Memories* No. 179 [p. 242]
24 Dorothea Herbert: *Recollections*, p. 203.
25 ib., p. 269.
26 *Memories* p. 242, n. 2.

Nuns and Monks at Hennessy's Road

Edmund Rice and the Presentation Sisters in Waterford.

Assumpta O'Neill, PBVM

To WRITE OF EDMUND RICE and the Presentation sisters and their mutual relationship requires that we do so against the background of their time and place, that is, in the context of Catholic life in Waterford in the closing years of the eighteenth century and the opening decades of the nineteenth. Specifically, it requires that we look at the provision, or lack of it, for education of the very poorest, in order to understand their preoccupation with providing schooling for all, especially the most destitute. This in turn entails taking into account the legislation then in place and how that legislation was or was not realised in practice.

Some clarification is also called for on the terminology. When Edmund Rice and his community of brothers lived in Mount Sion, they were commonly called 'monks' and their dwelling house, on the north side of Hennessy's Road, was known as the Monastery. The convent on the south side of Hennessy's Road had a community of nuns, and until the Brothers' Chapter of 1822, both communities were Presentation. After that date, Edmund Rice and his brothers decided to draw up their own rule, and took the title Brothers of the Christian Schools of Ireland, hence 'Christian Brothers', as they were popularly called. In Cork, a group of Edmund Rice's brothers decided to remain under diocesan jurisdiction.[1] They kept, and still keep, the title Presentation.

Edmund Rice interested himself in the affairs of several Presentation convents, as his letters show, and he was involved to some extent in the founding of a convent in Manchester in 1836. This essay, however, deals exclusively with the community in Waterford city, a community which kept his name so faithfully in memory that one of the Brothers felt moved to comment in 1912 "I learned more at the convent about the life and character of our

79

Founder than I ever knew before."[2] The decade of the 1790s was a dramatic one in Waterford, as indeed in all of Ireland. Its opening was marked by an optimism generated by the Relief Act of 1782 and by the conviction that a new era of freedom and equality was dawning. In 1793, the year of a further Relief Act, the River Suir at Waterford was bridged for the first time.[3] This physical, visible bridge-building was seen perhaps as a symbol of a new spirit of unity. The inscription on the new bridge began

"In 1793,
a year rendered sacred
to National Prosperity
by the extinction of Religious Divisions
the Foundation of this Bridge was laid."

The wording conveys the sense of hope for a future that would be free of the pain of the recent past. It looked as if the final decade of the eighteenth century had got off to a good start. A spirit of ecumenism was growing in Waterford. The exclusively Protestant Corporation made a grant to Catholics of a site for a new chapel. The architect, the Protestant John Roberts, had previously worked on the plans of the Protestant Cathedral. Catholic Emancipation looked likely to materialise in the very near future, certainly not later than 1800. The year 1795 saw the opening of Maynooth College for the education of Catholic clergy.[4] Yet a change was already threatening. Britain went to war with France in 1793 and the recall to London in 1795 of Viceroy Fitzwilliam after only six weeks in office was considered to be due to his overt wish for the immediate granting of Catholic Emancipation. A Union of the Parliaments of Britain and Ireland was mooted. Deep discontent began to stir among the people, and Wolfe Tone was goaded into abandoning his original idea of non-violent agitation to adopt the ideal of armed revolution, looking to the French model of 1789, which had in turn looked back to the American colonists of 1776.

This final decade of the eighteenth century was the decade which saw the beginnings of Presentation work in Waterford.[5] While great matters were being discussed and decided upon by the literate minority, the smelly, half-naked, hungry children of the lanes and tenements of the city were wandering in the desert of

80

hopeless and helpless penury.[6] It was to these that Edmund Rice's attention was drawn by a discerning friend after she had learned of his decision to enter religious life, following the death of his wife.[7] Once alerted to the needs that were crying out literally on his own doorstep, he did not hesitate for long. The earliest written source gives the year 1793 as the year when he took the first step in what was to be a lifelong journey.

When Brother Mark Hill began in 1912 his painstaking work of collecting memories of Edmund Rice from the people of Waterford, Kilkenny and elsewhere, he was advised one day by Bishop Sheehan to call to the Presentation Convent. The fact that the traditions regarding Edmund Rice were so alive at the convent nearly seventy years after his death is partly due to the particular history of the house. Set up in 1798, it had, in common with most other Presentation convents, remained an autonomous community ever since. Indeed there was a high degree of autonomy even in its beginnings. The nucleus of the Waterford community was made up of three Waterford ladies who went to Cork in 1795 to do their training in the ways of religious life and in the manner of conducting schools. Three years after their return to Waterford, the house set up its own novitiate and henceforth candidates who entered there spent the remainder of their lives in that same community.[8] In such a setting the passing on of oral tradition was bound to be part of the community ethos. Moreover, one of the nuns who gave such valuable testimony to Brother Mark was Sister Joseph Meagher, whose two aunts, Cahill sisters from Upperchurch in County Tipperary, had joined the Waterford community at Edmund's urging. According to Sister Joseph, one of them had intended entering the Presentation Convent in Killarney, the other the Ursuline Convent in Thurles, until Edmund, who was a family acquaintance and knew of their plans, persuaded them that Waterford needed themselves and their fortunes! He also added some practical advice on community living, telling them they should "hear and see and say nothing!" At the time they entered, one of them was a young widow whose late husband was surnamed Keeshan, and their memories live on under their religious names, Baptist Cahill and Patrick Keeshan. (It was customary until recent times for a woman to take at her profession the name of some patron saint, male or female. The significance was that the radical following of Christ involved in religious profession was parallel to the call of Simon, who became Peter, or Saul who became Paul. The new name was an important symbol of a new identity.) Some of the surviving letters of Edmund are addressed to one or other of these two sisters, who were at various times in charge of the community and its business affairs.

Further memories provided to Mark by the convent community regarded a man known affectionately in Waterford as "Black Johnnie". The story is that he came in to the port of Waterford on a trading vessel, and for some reason or other the Captain wanted to be rid of him or the boy wanted to be left ashore. At any rate the Captain agreed to hand him over to Edmund Rice. Presumably a 'ransom' was paid. The testimony says Edmund "negotiated with the Captain" for him. As a young lad, Johnnie became a messenger-boy for the nuns. In adult life, with Edmund's help, he prospered in business and became a property owner. In his will he bequeathed to the nuns two houses in Gallows Road, which they let to tenants William Sage and John Phelan at annual rents of £3.10s. and £4 respectively.[9]

Mark Hill was also told about a dramatic little incident related to Johnnie's death.[10] The nuns sent a woman to prepare his body for burial. She afterwards exclaimed at the convent "Black Johnnie's soul is as white as snow in heaven!" In our day, to use an epithet based on someone's skin-colour might be considered distasteful, but it was obviously not so in Black Johnnie's day. It was of the same sort as the many Irish epithets based on colour of hair – *an cailín deas donn, an páiste fionn, an fear rua.* Black Johnnie's 'legal' name was John Thomas and under this name he is listed among the benefactors of the Presentation Convent.

Another character in the story told to Brother Mark was one Poll Carty whose name had likewise lived on in the Presentation consciousness. It was a story they obviously enjoyed telling, since they returned to it on his second visit, leading Brother Mark to conclude that "they were impressed themselves by the case". The story as reported by Brother Mark is that "there was an old woman in Waterford who was a great drunkard. She resolved to take the pledge from Fr. Mathew in Cork.[11] She said that she would go to Br. Rice in Mount Sion. He gave her a habit. She put it on and walked to Cork, took the pledge, kept it and was most edifying for the remainder of her life".[12] After his next visit he added that "the woman was abandoned by every person when the founder

83

Presentation Convent Chapel, Waterford

Founder's Ciborium

Pathway to Presentation Convent, Hennessy's Road

took her in hand . . . He got the Presentation Nuns to instruct her, gave her a somewhat clerical costume which she wore on her way to and from Cork. In the written testimony drawn up and signed, it is discreetly given as "a dress which satisfied her".[13] On her return after walking the whole way barefoot,[14] she kept the pledge, led a most religious life and died a Saint".[15]

Poll Carty and Black Johnnie are more than individuals, they are types from the busy port-town which Waterford was in the early 1800s. Black Johnnie had the potential to make his way in the world, and the help of Edmund Rice enabled him to do so, as it enabled another immigrant, Charles Bianconi. They learned, too, that prosperity carries its own responsibilities, and both became benefactors of those less fortunate. Poll, on the other hand, like many of her sex and class, had very few friends indeed, but she obviously felt confident that some of them lived at Hennessy's Road. She never acquired material wealth, yet her story has continued to enrich others for almost two centuries.

One of the tantalising bits of information given to Brother Mark by the nuns was that they previously possessed "a letter or rather a lot of letters of our Founder", but they added that these had already been given to the Brothers. Unfortunately the exact details of where the letters ended up are unclear and remain so. The nuns thought the letters had been given in 1883, and various brothers were named as possible recipients, but no trace of the letters was found. Brother Mark was all the more anxious to trace them when he became convinced that "the Nuns seem to know more about him personally and to understand his character and aims better than we did."[16]

All unknown to Mark and probably to the two sisters (otherwise they would have mentioned them) was the existence of two short but important letters written by Edmund Rice in 1835 and 1839 respectively and addressed to the convent.[17] These two letters caused a little flurry of joy on their coming to light in the summer of 1985. For an unknown number of years, they had lain in a bureau drawer at the convent among a bundle of Share Certificates. In fact they were written on the reverse side of two of these Certificates, and are in many ways typical of Edmund's dealings with the Waterford sisters. There is meticulous attention to business and the fidelity to strict accountability. On the other hand is the personal touch "My dear Mary Patrick . . .," he begins. He confides the state of progress of the business which had taken him to Dublin. Such personal reporting whether on the state of his health or the state of business, was also characteristic of his correspondence with the sisters. Then comes what Brother John E. Carroll has called "a little jewel of otherwordliness.[18] "But we must wait for God's time," writes Edmund, in a phrase which is almost an echo of Nano Nagle's "we must believe the Almighty does everything for the best." Finally the letters end with a warm greeting to the community – "my love to all the sisters. Yours most affectionately, Edmund I. Rice."

The little bundle of Share Certificates is in itself a reminder of the many occasions when Edmund Rice's business sense and financial expertise were put to use for the benefit of the sisters. In June 1796, he took a lease of a site on the south side of Hennessy's Road in the city. On this site the convent was built. The early account books of the convent, now in the archives, are partly in the handwriting of Edmund and of Bishop John Power.[19] Edmund signed the wills of eleven of the early sisters: he invested their dowries, and generally acted as their business manager and agent of their affairs. Even such a mundane detail as a supply of cocoa appears in Edmund's writing on the 1825 page of the Cash Book. As each new recruit joined the community, an account had to be kept of her boarding fee for the period of her novitiate. These also are in Edmund's writing.

The convent and the 'monastery' of Mount Sion were eventually both built, one on each side of Hennessy's Road.[20] One chaplain served both and the Brothers attended Mass daily at the convent chapel,[21] where the Profession ceremony of the first Brothers took place on 15 August, 1808. Seven brothers took their vows "according to the rules and constitutions of the Congregation of nuns of the Presentation of Our Blessed Lady . . . until the sanction of the Holy See shall be obtained to make them in a Congregation of Religious men of the Presentation of our Blessed Lady." What was important for Edmund was that when he did come to form his own Congregation, he did not have to search for an appropriate Rule of Life. Such a search had occupied Nano for years, involving correspondence with various continental congregations.[22] She did not find one to coincide with her dreams for a new Congregation and eventually, after her death, a Rule of Life for her sisters was drawn up by a Franciscan, Laurence

Callanan, who also suggested the title 'Presentation'.[23] Laurence Callanan, described by the Presentation annalist as "a man filled with the Spirit of God" was Nano's spiritual guide during her last years and continued after her death to interest himself in the affairs of the struggling Congregation. His work in Ireland, where he had care of the Province, involved him in much travelling. In summer 1791, for example, he visited Galway. Later that same year he was at Waterford. The following year he went to Athlone and Wexford. In December 1793, he was in Cork (his "base", since he was Superior of the Community there as well as being Provincial).[24] It is tempting to speculate whether he was the friar with whom on one of his travels, Edmund Rice shared a hotel room and was so inspired by the friar's prayerfulness that he "resolved from the example set to him to give himself more to prayer and to lead a monk's life of retirement and contemplation".[25] Whether it was Laurence Callanan or some other friar, the encounter made a lasting impression on Edmund, who confided it to the Presentation sisters in such a way that they interpreted it as "his own account of the circumstances which led him to devote his life to the service of God."[26]

The Rule drawn up by Laurence Callanan was a re-writing of the earlier Rule of Bishop Moylan. The latter expressly stated that he had written on the basis of the lifestyle he witnessed among Nano and her companions. Laurence Callanan's Rule is therefore in a strict sense Nano's Rule, embodying not just her ideals but their lived expression. This Rule was available to Edmund through the Waterford sisters and was used by him and the first Brothers until their General Chapter of 1822. The Presentation Brothers continued to use it until 1967. The Sisters of Mercy at their origin used it with the addition of a single chapter (on visitation of the sick and needy).

In their testimony to Mark Hill, in 1912, the sisters laid no great stress on the influence their community had on Edmund Rice. They are much more aware, it is clear, of the great kindness shown by him in so many practical ways. "Brother Rice assisted the nuns in every possible way . . . he assisted the Convent by giving the nuns financial help . . . he directed [the two Cahill sisters] to join the Presentation Convent, Waterford . . . the nuns have a lovely table which was presented by Brother Rice . . . it showed his appreciation . . . it indicated the generosity of Brother Rice . . .

the Presentation nuns of Waterford had a personal knowledge of Brother Rice for more than 40 years . . . Brother Rice helped the nuns very much . . . he was very charitable and pious and could see no one in want without assisting him if he possibly could . . . he and his early companions gave the Presentation nuns much valuable help in the management of their schools."[27] Only once do they refer to the possibility that he may have seen something inspiring, something worthy of imitation, in the lives of the nuns. "The lives of the Presentation Nuns must also have been very suggestive to Brother Rice to further Christian and secular education, particularly in regard to the poor."[28]

Yet there is a contemporary source which gives much more weight than this to the influence on Edmund of the Presentation Sisters' life and work. In the course of a long sermon given at Waterford Cathedral in October, 1844, the preacher had this to say: "Some years before the foundation of the Christian Schools, the labours of the Ladies of the Presentation Order were felt and appreciated . . . I speak but the truth when I say that the elevation of the female character in Ireland is, in a great measure, attributable to their generous and disinterested labours. They have another claim on our lasting gratitude: it is this; that it was their noble example that stimulated Edmund Rice to share in their meritorious labours. In this city he witnessed the blessings which poor females derived from the truly Christian education they imparted . . . He too would rescue the poor friendless boy from the misery and degradation to which ignorance and bad example must have led him." The occasion of this sermon was the Month's Mind for Edmund Rice and the preacher was Reverend Richard Fitzgerald, confessor to the Brothers for seventeen years who had, in his own words, "the privilege of preparing that great and holy man for death". He could therefore be expected to know Edmund's mind on this aspect of the inspiration for his life's work. The sermon was printed in Dublin as a pamphlet in that same year 1844, and was reprinted in 1863, 1864, and 1902.[29] Seventeen years later, in 1861, an appeal on behalf of the Presentation Sisters was printed in the *Waterford Citizen*. The writer was Dr. James Vincent Cleary.[30] He states "the very existence of their Institute was a constant demand for a counterpart to supply education to the male youth of Ireland; and it is an historical fact, that the success which attended the efforts of the Presentation Nuns in this city, first suggested to the ever-venerable Edmund Rice the happy thought of founding the Congregation of Christian Brothers, the most laborious and most useful body of men on the face of the earth."

In more recent times, Brother A. L. O'Toole who wrote exhaustively on Edmund's life and work, presents a detailed analysis of the various motivating circumstances for Edmund Rice's decision to dedicate his life to the education of the poor. He too, considers the influence of the Sisters to be decisive, but he sees it active even before the nuns opened their school in Waterford. He noted that the earliest written source for Edmund's life dated the beginning of his educational apostolate to the year 1793.[31] That would coincide approximately with the date when a plan was conceived to set up a Presentation convent in the city of Waterford.[32] Brother O'Toole also drew attention to the fact that 1793 was the year when Fr. Laurence Callanan completed the writing of the Rule for the sisters in Cork. In general, his argument seems to be that Edmund was aware of developments in Cork even before the Presentation Order spread to Waterford. He quotes a Mount Sion tradition to the effect that Edmund resolved to do for the poor neglected boys of Waterford 'what Miss Nano Nagle had just done for the poor girls of the city of Cork.'[33] As early as 1769, Nano was able to write 'My schools are beginning to be of service to a great many parts of the world – this is a place of such trade – my views are not for one object alone – if I could be of service in saving souls in any part of the world, I would willingly do all in my power.' The following year, she wrote 'I am sending boys to the West Indies. Some charitable gentlemen put themselves to great expense . . . all my children are brought up to be fond of instructing . . . they promise me they will take great pains with the little blacks to instruct them . . . next year I will have pictures for them that go to give the Negroes . . .' With such a world-scheme in operation by 1770, it would be surprising indeed if the work of Nano was unknown in Waterford in the 1790s. She herself visited the city on at least one occasion, and lodged at a house in Patrick Street, where a commemorative wall-plaque hung until the house was demolished in 1973.[34] Her visit is quite likely to have had something to do with her work for the schools, as she made it a rule, as she said, never to travel for any other reason. Of her visit to her brothers in Bath in the summer of 1770, she wrote 'it

89

was so much against my inclination to leave my children, and only to serve the foundation I never should have prevailed on myself'. Certainly, some of Nano's protegées in Cork found employment in Waterford, as is clear from an entry in the Annals of South Presentation Convent. 'A poor girl, reared up in our schools, was necessitated to quit her home and to accept some lowly situation in the City of Waterford . . .' As no date is given for the girl's arrival in Waterford, it does not settle any questions of chronology, but the story goes on to say that it was the life of this anonymous evangelist that drew attention to what was happening in Cork. Whether it was in fact the first intimation of it we cannot know, but she was the personification of it and as such had an impact that surpassed any hearsay.

The story of Edmund Rice and the Presentation Sisters is a story of co-operation rather than of competition, of mutually enriching partnership, in short, a story of friendship. The relationship was, and continued to be one of equality, evidenced in the ease and freedom of their dialogue. On one occasion, in answer to the nuns' request to have a ciborium brought to them from Dublin on his next visit there, he good-humouredly replied 'You are excellent beggars.'[35] They, in their turn, felt quite free to reprimand him when they considered that they had not got their fair share of the spiritual assistance of Peter Kenny, S.J., when he was at Mount Sion in 1813. It appears indeed that they were well able to voice their discontent whenever things were not to their liking. Edmund remarked in a letter to the Sisters at George's Hill, Dublin 'Your sisters here are all very well; they say we are the cause of keeping Mr. Kenny from them, but this is their usual mode of acting, as when anything goes amiss with them, if possible some of the blame must fall on us'.[36] When, later on, the sisters learned that Edmund Rice and his brothers were preparing to set up a central administration, they sought assurance that they would not be expected to become dependent members, 'as the Daughters of St. Vincent are to the Superiors of the Priests of the Mission'.[37] Whether their fears were well-founded we do not know, but at any rate they were not realized.

The central preoccupation of both the Mount Sion brothers and the Presentation sisters was to 'respond to the voice of the unheard as they cry out to be liberated from enslavement.'[38] The earliest Constitutions of the sisters has the first chapter headed 'On the particular purpose of this institute, or on the vow of instruction of poor girls', while the 1809 Constitutions very clearly state 'What is particularly characteristic of this institute is a most serious application to the instruction of poor female children in the principles of religion and Christian piety'. Edmund Rice used this rule, as we have already seen, and in his act of profession in 1808 uses the words 'for the instruction of poor boys'. In 1821, Archbishop Murray of Dublin wrote "The Brother Monks did the same work for poor boys which the nuns were doing for poor girls." An appeal by the Brothers in 1829 clearly states that "the object for which these Brothers have associated is the Gratuitous Education of the Poor."[39]

Attempts to set up schools for the poor had gone on all through the eighteenth century. There was a whole state system of parish, charter, diocesan and royal schools, created by a series of enactments starting in Tudor times. "These schools were to have ensured the conversion of Roman Catholics to Protestantism and the control of education by the established Church. Neither objective had been achieved, so that by the last quarter of the eighteenth century the official school system served only the Protestant population while Roman Catholics patronised an extensive pay school system, over which Roman Catholic parish priests were able to assert a considerable degree of control."[40] However modest the fee charged in these pay schools, there were hundreds who simply could not afford to pay. As late as 1825, there were over twenty such schools in Waterford. They are described by the Commissioners for Education in their Report of that year. Accommodation varied. A mud cabin in Yellow Road catered for 65 pupils at a cost each of "2d to 6d weekly". In Trinity Lane there was "a wretched room" where 15 pupils were taught. Here the fee was "2d to 4d" a week. Fifteen others paid 3s 3d to 4s 4d a quarter in another "wretched room", this time in Queen Street. In Arundel Lane, pupils in "a room in a wretched lodging house" were charged 3d a week. Tuition was gratis at the Christian Brothers' school, at the Presentation school and at the poor school in the Ursuline Convent. This Report of 1825 was edited by J. O'Flynn in the Catholic Record of Waterford and Lismore for March, 1918.

What of Waterford a quarter of a century earlier? Bishop Hussey of Waterford wrote from London in June 1797 to

Dean Hearn "How do the schools for the instruction of the poor succeed?" And in his next letter he again asks how the conferences and the poor schools go on. "They are objects of the greatest importance." Five months later he is still concerned. "I hope that the different Charity Schools in the diocese are properly attended to by the respective Pastors, and the Parochial Committees formed for the purpose." Not until September 1799 does the Dean reply to the questions. "My brother and I called together yesterday a good many of our people in order to enter into subscriptions for establishing poor schools, and the plan has met the universal approbation of all present, so that we are busy now in procuring school houses for the poor children of both sexes: I took the liberty of mentioning your name as one who would encourage such an establishment." And he adds "What may I promise towards it from you?"! His own meagre donation of £5 he excuses on the grounds that the "chapel" (i.e. the Cathedral), then in the course of construction had "beggared him."

In a letter which must have crossed with this as it was written from London only three days later, Dr. Hussey remarks "You do not say a word of the convent lately established in Waterford for the instruction of the poor". Hearn's reply to this is not very enthusiastic! But he goes on to thank the Bishop for his "liberal subscription to our poor school; I hope it will take well; my brother is indefatigable in promoting it, and we have already a long list of subscribers; this day we meet, to choose teachers, male and female, and to look out for proper school rooms; may God grant us peace and good neighbourhood to pursue so good an institution but alas! I fear we must wade through more trials before so happy an object will be attained."

This dialogue covering two years 1797-9 is important for two reasons. It clearly conveys the reality of the situation with regard to the provision of schools for the poor, theoretically in operation by then in every parish. In so doing, it throws light on the role of Edmund Rice and of the Presentation Sisters. Certainly in Waterford there was no developed system of parochial schools under lay management, as is clear from the above correspondence. W. G. Healy, writing of Kilkenny in the second half of the eighteenth century remarks, "Schools came and went after a few years." His opinion is that the pay-schools were often "little more than desperate attempts to make a living."

He instances one gentleman who, failing to obtain employment as a butler, advertised himself as a schoolmaster.[41] This is the context to Nano's discontent with those who did the work [of teaching] "only for bread". (Letter dated 24 August, 1778.) This is a comment on the economic and social reality of her time.

Dean Hearn's pride in his new Cathedral is tangible in his correspondence with Dr. Husssey. "Our chapel, I hope will surprise you. Our altar is advanced to the bases of the pillars together with railing and sanctuary: the chapel is entirely floored and the sacristy finished, so that we have now our Masses in it every day and have bid adieu to the little chapel which is, by its pastor's endeavours, in very neat order."[42] Toleration for Catholics allowed them to become visible once more, and for Dean Hearn that visibility was being expressed in a fine new 'chapel', which absorbed not only his funds but much of his time and energy. Bishop Hussey, on the other hand, was deeply interested in education at all levels. He was the first President of Maynooth College, and he was instrumental in having the continental colleges re-opened for the training of clergy.

When Bishop Hussey died in 1803, he was succeeded by John Power, Parish Priest of St. John's, who continued to support wholeheartedly the Presentation schools. As already mentioned, he had been one of the main agents in introducing the Presentation work to Waterford in the first place. His funeral in 1816 was attended by "practically every citizen of Waterford including the Protestant Bishop and clergy".[43] The spirit of ecumenism had come alive again in Waterford.

When Edmund Rice began what was to become his life's main work, he gathered a few ragged boys in a stable loft in New Street. Forty years before, when Nano began in Cove Lane in Cork, she gave the outside of the building the appearance of a bread-shop. There is something striking about the symbols – the house of bread, the 'bethlehem', the stable, the small weak beginnings, the mustard seed which Nano herself used as a symbol in one of her few direct Scripture-references. At the convent in Waterford can be seen a related symbol – the silver ciborium brought from Dublin by Edmund at the nuns' request. It is unadorned, functional even, but of generous size, and continues to be in regular use in the sacramental 'House of Bread' where the hungry of spirit can buy food without price and are nourished into newness of life.

A Man Raised Up

References

1 This arrangement no longer obtains.
2 Brother Mark Hill to the Provincial in a letter dated 30 April, 1912, printed in *Educational Record*, 1986, p. 53.
3 This bridge, known affectionately as 'Old Timbertoes' from its piers of oaks, served its purpose until its replacement in 1911. It was a toll bridge. Funerals however were free, and it was notable that they were very well attended! The present bridge is named Rice Bridge, in honour of a Kilkennyman!
4 J. Newman, *Maynooth and Georgian Ireland* (Kenny's Galway 1979).
5 Under the title "Presentation Work", I include both the sisters and the brothers.
6 Thackeray's description of Cork's "alleys where the odours and rags and the darkness are so hideous, that one runs frightened away from them" would be equally apt in Waterford.
7 *Edmund Ignatius Rice and the Christian Brothers* by A Christian Brother, p. 70. M. H. Gill & Son (Dublin) 1926.
8 Exceptions were those four who left to help establish houses in Dungarvan (1809), Clonmel (1813), Carrick-on-Suir (1813) and Lismore (1836).
9 Account-books in convent archives, Waterford.
10 He died 15 February, 1848.
11 For a brief but comprehensive account of Fr. Theobald Mathew, his life and work, see M. Lysaght, *Fr. Theobald Mathew* (Four Courts Press, 1985). He was related to Nano Nagle through her mother, Anne Mathew (p.13).
12 Letter dated 30 April, 1912.
13 *Memories* p.269.
14 The double journey would be about 160 miles.
15 Letter dated 11 May, 1912.
16 Letter dated 1 May, 1912.
17 These letters are not listed in the official documentation drawn up by Br. Normoyle, as they were unknown.
18 *Educational Record*, 1986, p. 136. Brother J. E. Carroll wrote a comprehensive analysis of the letters and their context. I am indebted to him for the insight I am using here, as well as for continuing to share on our charisms and their similarities.
19 John Power as P.P. of St. John's was instrumental in setting up the Waterford community. He provided them with accommodation for the first six weeks after they returned from Cork. Later on, as successor to Bishop Thomas Hussey, he encouraged and supported them in every way.
20 'Monastery' was used as a designation for the Brothers' dwelling-house. A table which Edmund Rice gave to the Presentation nuns has the inscription underneath "Mr. Rice, Monastery." 'Mount Sion' is said to have been the suggestion of Bishop Hussey, because its elevated position reminded him of Jerusalem.
21 *Memories* p.263.
22 See Nano's Letters; also the analysis of the search for a Rule in J. J. Walsh, *Nano Nagle and the Presentation Sisters*; p. 101 ff. also Raphael Considine, *Listening Journey*, pp.71 – 3.
23 Walsh, op. cit. p.102.
24 Louvain Papers (ed. B. Jennings) nos. 698, 699, 701, 703, 704, 707.
25 *Memories* p.266.
26 *Memories* p.366.
27 ibid., p.267-9.
28 ibid., p. 267
29 This information I received from Brother John E. Carroll, CFC.
30 Professor, and later President, of St. John's College, he was appointed Bishop of

Nuns and Monks at Hennessy's Road

Kingston, Canada in 1880. L. J. Flynn in *The Story of the Roman Catholic Church in Kingston 1826-1976*, p. 69, describes him as "one of the great intellects of his time in Canada", whose "pastoral and doctrinal letters are recognised as literary masterpieces." A portrait of him hangs in the Community Room at Waterford convent, in acknowledgement of his many benefactions to the nuns.

31 A. L. O'Toole CFC *A Spiritual Profile of Edmund Ignatius Rice* (Burleigh Press, Bristol, 1984), p. 71.

32 Three ladies left Waterford for Cork on 1 April, 1795 to commence their training in South Presentation. It is not unreasonable to suppose that this move was preceded by lengthy planning and preparation.

33 O'Toole, op. cit. p. 78. Interestingly, the tradition makes no mention of the fact that Nano also had schools for boys. See Walsh, op. cit. p. 78. Nano's own account of the circumstances which led to her involvement in the education of boys is told in her letter of 17 July, 1769.

34 The account of her visit I had from Miss Toni O'Neill of Tramore who lived at the house in Patrick Street and remembered the plaque clearly. She does not know what became of it when the house was demolished.

35 *Memories*, p. 267

36 Letter dated 2 November, 1813.

37 M. C. Normoyle (ed.) *A Tree is Planted*, p. 124.

38 This phrase is a quotation from Terence McCaughey, *Memory and Redemption*, p. 95-6.

39 M. C. Normoyle, *The Roman Correspondence*, p. 145

40 This is the assessment of Harold Hislop in an article entitled "The 1806-12 Board of Education and Non-Denominational Education in Ireland" in OIDEAS, Earrach 1993.

41 W. G. Healy, *Kilkenny* (Institute of Irish Studies QUB, 1989).

42 Hussey-Hearn Correspondence, Diocesan Archives in Bishop's House, Waterford.

43 P. Power Waterford and Lismore (Longman, Green & Co., 1937), p. 36.

Edmund Rice – A Timely Restorer of Faith and Hope in Ireland

Daniel V. Kelleher, CFC

IN THE HISTORY of any nation certain people make a profound impact, their influence being outstanding in the life of the people. Desmond Rushe would consider that Daniel O'Connell, Fr. Mathew and Edmund Rice were such people.[1] Edmund's congregation was to forge a defence against the greatest of all dangers at that time for the soul of the nation: Evangelism. High stakes were at issue at this critical moment in Irish history.

With the first relaxation of the Penal Laws the Catholic Church in the towns was faced with a situation calling for heroic measures. The humble beginnings of the religious teaching congregations particularly the Presentation Nuns and the Christian Brothers gave cause for hope that eventually the problem of education would be solved. Without the possibility of material advantage, men and women came forward and met the needs of a time in perhaps the only adequate way – the complete dedication of their lives. Even as late as 1824 the numbers of children in these schools were but a fraction of the whole, but their example inspired others and helped to infuse into the Catholic community a much needed sense of significance and confidence. The great devotion of these religious, both men and women, to the work of education, their methods of instruction and school organisation, their high ideals and obvious influence for good, won the unstinted admiration of all unbiased observers. They laid down an early framework of an Irish educational system.

Catholic education for the poor was practically non-existent. In common with other cities, Waterford had its share of private academies catering for the wealthier sections of the community, proselytising schools against which Dr. Hussey, the Bishop, directed his pastoral of 1797. These were the Charter Schools at Killotran.[2] just outside the city and catering for 50 or 60 boys and girls, the Bishop Foy School[3] with 75 boys and the Blue Coat School for 34 girls.[4] Consequently in Waterford, in 1800, there could not have been much more than 350 Catholic children at school irrespective of the type of school. Between four and five thousand Catholic children were running wild in the streets; but Waterford was neither better nor worse than most of the cities and towns of Ireland at the time. It was to remedy this situation, the direct result of the Penal Laws, that religious congregations in Ireland sprang up.

Compared with the complexity of the law, the immensity of the task was a straightforward difficulty. By 1802, Mr. Rice had definitely decided to devote himself and his talents, and wealth to the cause of education but before commencing, mere caution would suggest that he find a way to safeguard his property for the work. His capitalised assets were in the region of £50,000,[5] a not inconsiderable sum for those times.

The greatest obstacle facing Mr. Rice at the time was contained in the Act of 1791.[6] This act contained a section opposing the establishment of any religious order or society, bound by monastic vows. Even though Mr. Rice, in 1802, when he opened his first school, did not have specifically in mind, the founding of a religious Society, nevertheless, events soon turned his thoughts in that direction. However, the Act of 1791 seemed to place an insurmountable barrier in his way. The actual wording of the Act on this point is very clear and it furthermore re-affirms the penalising Clause of the 1782 Act against endowments. The relevant section ran:

> Provided also be it further enacted that nothing in this Act contained shall make it lawful to found, endow or establish any religious Order or Society of persons bound by monastic or religious vows: or to found, endow or establish any School, Academy or College by persons professing the Catholic Religion within the realms or the Dominions thereunto belonging; and that all uses, trusts and dispositions, whether real or personal property, which, immediately before the said 24th day of June, 1791 shall be deemed superstitious or unlawful, shall continue to be deemed and taken, anything in this Act to the contrary notwithstanding.

When Nano Nagle started her society of sisters, in 1775, there was no legal prohibition preventing her from doing so. The act of 1791 contained, for the first time, a positive prohibition against the founding of such societies, in Ireland, and even in the very Act of Emancipation in 1829, these clauses against male religious societies were repeated.

Mr. Rice's work for education was inspired by his love of God and his neighbour, and as a consequence, his attitude on the religious training of his pupils was uncompromising. He gave up all to carry out a certain ideal and the type of education given in his schools was firmly based upon the principles of the Catholic Church. The school atmosphere was to be a religious atmosphere and even secular lessons, where appropriate, were to be directed to this end. The later schools of the National Board did not measure up to these standards and, except for a brief period on trial, the Brothers never had any connection with the National Board. To safeguard the principles and ideals of their Founder, the Christian Brothers, at great financial loss, remained outside all State-aided systems of education, until the setting up of two governments, at the time of Partition, made it possible for them to come into the State system without losing any of their traditional approach to education. Mr. Rice's schools were in complete harmony with a full Catholic tradition and as such were completely opposed to the countless schools, scriptural and otherwise which were being, and were to be, all too persuasively urged upon Irish Catholics. The schools of the Christian Brothers kept before the people, the type of school in keeping with a full Catholic heritage and prevented a too great complacency with the schools sponsored by the state. Any Christian Brothers' school, at the present time, that puts religion in a lowly position has betrayed the purpose for its foundation.

By means of night classes, Mr. Rice and his two companions came into contact with the young men of Waterford, teaching them how to read and instructing them in the fundamentals of Christian belief and practice. It was customary at that time for non-Catholic schools to offer food, clothing and sometimes money to Catholic children who attended. These were often in the nature of a bribe. The children were so poor with the ragged clothing and hungry looks, that anything in the way of food and clothing was a great charity. Unfortunately, attendance at non-Catholic schools was so often the usual condition that the charity became suspect. At Mount Sion, Mr. Rice provided free meals every day for the poorest of pupils, and for many years he kept a tailor in constant employment to supply new clothing and repair the old. This became a common feature in most of the subsequent establishments opened by him.[7]

After the initial hardships and experiences, a system of education was worked out which has stood the test of time. With religion at its core, a well-balanced curriculum was followed and the results, even academically, were of a high order. There is no need to enlarge on this aspect of things.

The laws against endowing Catholic schools and against the founding of monastic societies were still on the statute book but circumstances seemed to warrant that harsh measures would not be resorted to. Napoleon was practically master of Europe and England was fighting for survival. The granting of the franchise to the Catholics in 1793, had given to them some measure of political importance, and the growing spirit of toleration and goodwill at home made persecution seem unlikely. In addition, the people of Waterford, Protestant as well as Catholic, had nothing but admiration for the work being done by Mr. Rice and his fellow workers. Sir John Newport, the parliamentary representative of Waterford, fully shared the admiration for the work being done and moreover was a personal friend·of Edmund Rice. It was in Waterford that the first petition demanding equal rights for Catholics originated.[8] Petitions followed from all over the country and Lord Granville and Henry Grattan presented them to Parliament. Even though debates came to naught, an assurance was given by the British Government of an honourable spirit of toleration towards the Catholics of Ireland.

Edmund Rice was now satisfied that there would be no repercussion to the carrying out of the second stage of his plan – the consolidation of his little Society by obtaining the preliminary sanction of the Church. Accordingly, he applied to the Bishop for permission to take the vows of poverty, chastity and obedience, both for himself and for those of his colleagues who wished to do so.[9] They may seem foreign to education, but in reality they were to Edmund Rice matters of the first moment in the cause of education; and so he sought and obtained the approval of the Holy See.

An officially sanctioned society has greater permanency and stability than individual effort and has a greater attraction for those who wish to devote themselves to the particular work in hand. But for the official approval of the Church, the work of Edmund Rice would, most likely, have ended with his death.

Dr. Power decided to give Br. Rice and his companions a clear distinctive religious dress and put him on the road to forming his new society. Thus by 1820, there were ten different establishments working in five dioceses and as the Brothers were following the Presentation rule at the time, innumerable difficulties soon arose. According to the Presentation rule, each house was a separate unit, directly subject to the local bishop. No transfers could be made from one house to another, without the consent of the bishop, the community council and the person involved. In addition, each house had its own funds and in theory was to recruit its own members. When Mr. Rice's Society began to spread, all the difficulties inherent in such a system became apparent. What was required was complete self-government, a central fund, and a central novitiate. It was due, in no small measure, to the help and advice of Dr. Murray that the new institute overcame these difficulties and attained the desired unity of government.

Whatever the sincerity of individuals, the whole tenor of the times in Ireland was weighed against producing a scheme of things satisfactory to the Catholics. Due to the determined opposition of George III, the Catholics failed on three occasions(1795, 1801, 1807) to win redress of their grievances. After 1809, opposition to Catholic claims was the first condition of office and the party, which in 1807 so pledged itself, was to dominate English politics until 1830.[10] The question of "Managing Ireland" was no longer that of managing the English colony in Ireland but of controlling the newly emerging Irish Nation.

In the face of the crisis, the ruling aristocracy had given over its pretension to independence and placed itself at the disposal of a new militantly anti-Catholic Ascendancy which played its cards well during the Regency crisis, strengthened its hand with the defeat of Fitzwilliam and with the passing of the Act of Union in 1800, held all the trumps. The English Government was content to leave things in their hands in Ireland, while at home it was officially opposed to Catholic Emancipation and made the maintenance of Protestant Ascendancy its vowed aim. Under such circumstances, education could not be but affected.

History, politics and religion were so inextricably interwoven in the Ireland of the nineteenth century, that it is well nigh impossible to differentiate between the political and the religious driving force of the education societies. Perhaps, it is unwise to make such distinctions. The state religion of the crown was the means of pacifying and dominating the colonies. It does seem, however, that those societies in receipt of parliamentary grants were being utilised by Government for political ends. It was blatant proselytism under the guise of education.

In 1801 the Association for Discountenancing Vice and Promoting the Knowledge and Practice of the Christian Religion (hereafter referred to as the Association), which was established in 1792, obtained a small parliamentary grant which they determined to use to aid in the building and maintaining of parish schools. Official policy, in so far as there was any official educational policy, was always opposed to the independent common pay-schools, now becoming increasingly more numerous and could always be counted upon to support any scheme which held even a modicum of hope that these common schools could be supplanted by 'safer' ones or that their pupils could be drawn into a system capable of control. The Parish schools of Henry VIII and their newly-found supporters in the Association were too Protestant in character and too intimately connected with the State-Church to raise any sanguine hopes that Catholics would flock to them.

Official educational policy was, for political reasons, aimed at control over the education of Catholics. The government was not prepared to make any concessions. Furthermore all the educational legislation, to date, recognised the supremacy of the State-Church in the matter and no Tory Government was prepared to draw up a scheme which would involve a head-on collision with the Establishment. In addition from 1800, and even before, a great wave of zeal for spreading the Bible swept Ireland and henceforth the reading of the Sacred Scriptures became, not only the one common essential in all the schemes of the societies, but also became the source of a bitter religious and educational controversy which raged during the first three decades of the nineteenth century.

During the first quarter of the nineteenth century, Ireland was overrun by various societies offering a type of education totally or partially unacceptable to Irish Catholics. "Common Christianity" became the fashionable phrase of the day. The activity of these societies was made possible by the eagerness of the people to provide education for their children, and the inability of many to pay for it. Whether stated or not, the tendency of these societies was opposed, in spirit and operation, to the religion, culture and traditions of the majority and their educational programme was heavily biased in that direction. Some, like the Kildare Place Society, would have denied any such implication and would have stoutly defended their system of education from any trace of interference with the religious beliefs of Catholics. What was intended to be neutral when viewed from a certain angle need not necessarily be so when viewed from another. This was the position in Ireland. The men responsible for the policy and organisation of these societies were by upbringing and conviction, so foreign to anything Catholic and so influenced by the monopoly of privilege and property that even the most sincere of them could hardly be expected to produce, for Catholics, an acceptable system of education. Little trouble was ever taken to bridge the gap. Unfortunately, the position was not quite so simple as that of one class failing to appreciate adequately the needs of another.

This rise of Evangelicalism was a phenomenon of the times which did much to complicate the educational question. In contrast to the official policy, which was in the main political with religious overtones, the aim of the societies to which the evangelical movement gave birth was religious reformation. They sought quite explicitly, the conversion of Irish Catholics through the instrumentality of the Bible. During the early part of the nineteenth century Irish Protestantism underwent a change. Previous theology and piety were proving unsatisfactory for some and the evangelical movement, originating in England, was the result. Widespread rationalism with the consequent obscuring of revelation brought about a reaction. The bible brought grace and the saving truths of salvation. Individual responsibility for the religious salvation of one's neighbour was the practical outcome of the evangelical movement. Evangelical fervour spread and gained in respectability influencing both the Church of Ireland and the Presbyterians.

As evangelicalism was more a matter of tone and emphasis, than a precise creed, it is difficult to estimate its influence on the Church of Ireland. But judging by the output and content of the theology writing at the period, there can be no doubt that evangelicalism was the predominating force. Catholicism was the great barrier between the Irish Catholic and the undiluted Christianity of the Gospels. Every effort was made to reach across the abyss of 'superstitious dogma' and present the unadorned truths of religion.

Between 1800 and 1830, no less than five national societies were set up to minister to the spiritual needs of the Irish: The Hibernian Bible Society (1806), The London Hibernian Society (1806), The Irish Society (1818), the Religious Tract and Book Society(1810), and the Sunday School Society(1809). These societies together with the Presbyterian Home Mission, the Baptists' Irish Society and the Irish Evangelical Society, an interdenominational body, concentrated, through schools, tracts and the distribution of the Bible, on wearing down the resistance of the Irish Catholic.[11] Naturally, education is one of the main departments of political philosophy as the powers of government and the rights of subjects are equally affected by the systems enforced or allowed to exist in a country, whether that country's institutions are free or independent of state aid or control. In all aspects consensus was easy except in the moral or the religious principles (what was for most of them the same thing) in which the next generation was to be brought up.

Resurgent Catholicism emerging from a century of persecution and slowly winning back civil equality collided violently with a resurgent Protestantism revived by Evangelicalism. The ensuing conflict led to bad feeling fomented by a spate of pamhleteering and public debates.[12] Education became a cock-pit. Dissensions among the Catholic body in Ireland and England arising out of the proposed Catholic Bill in 1813 and the subsequent controversy over the Quarantotti Rescript focused Catholic attention elsewhere, but by 1818 the danger threatening the Catholic Church was realised for what it was. To Catholic leaders, it must have appeared that one vast conspiracy had sprung up.

The Catholic hierarchy and clergy met the challenge and denounced, as opposed to Catholic teaching, the principles inherent in the private interpretation of the Scripture. Under this head, the education work of the various non-Catholic societies was condemned by the hierarchy. It is against some such background as that sketched above that the work of Edmund Rice must be studied.

The Association for Discountenancing Vice was the first of the Protestant societies to devote itself to education. After 1791 the Established Clergy made greater efforts to set up schools. For this resurgence the work of the Association must be given credit. It was founded in 1792 for the express purpose of 'Discountenancing vice' (which term was meant to cover the various forms of disloyalty and unrest among the people) and for promoting the knowledge and practice of the Christian religion as by law established. In all likelihood, the rise of the Association was influenced by recent events in France and its earliest work of distributing the Bible and moral tracts may be regarded as a counter-measure against disaffection. Feeling in Ireland was running high in 1792. Thus from the outset, the work of the Association was coloured by political overtones which did not lessen with the passage of the years. Ireland had two 'nations' or groups of people who maintained different religious mentalities. They lived in different cultures. Both 'nations' chose to reinforce their cultures by separate education in which they would be taught the history of their Volk.

It was not until 1801 that the Association, after becoming incorporated and receiving a parliamentary grant of £300, took up educational work through the medium of schools. Part of their funds were henceforth to be used to support the parochial schools of 28 Henry VIII and 7 William III. The conditions upon which aid was to be granted seemed to be expressly designed to further the intentions and overcome the vagueness of these Acts, which made no provision towards the cost of erecting schools or the payment of salaries. The Association was prepared to aid the erection of school houses by grants of money totalling half the amount of private subscription and in any event not exceeding £50

> to be paid as soon as a lease, or grant of one acre of ground in perpetuity for the purpose, shall be granted and registered[13] and the property vested in the State-Church.[14] An annual salary of £10, later increased to £12, with a bonus of £5, later £6, was to be paid to each teacher if the local Protestant minister and three or more subscribers approved the teacher's work.[15] Teachers had to be members of the State-Church, teach the Scriptures and the Church of Ireland catechism.[16]
>
> Essentially, a state-church organisation, the Association nevertheless, was not regarded by the Catholics with suspicion.

This did not mean approval. Due to its open avowal of its principles, no one was left in doubt.

Despite its strict Protestant organisation, the schools were frequented by Catholic children who had perforce to comply with the conditions as laid down:

All must read the Sacred Scriptures, but none excepting those who belong to the Establishcd Church are called upon to receive instruction in catechism of that Church, the only one allowed to be taught.[17]

Catholics sought admission to these schools. Public money was used to exploit, even indirectly, the inability of many Catholics to pay for the education of their children. This argument became all the more compelling when used against the Kildare Place Society which received considerable Parliamentary grants for the education of the poor.

Commenting upon the diminished proportion of Catholics to Protestants in and after 1823, the Association's *Report for 1824* says:

The diminished proportion of Roman Catholics to Protestants in the two latter years is easily accounted by the fact, known to all, that from the year 1820, the Roman Catholic clergy have been endeavouring not only to found schools peculiar to themselves, but in many instances to withdraw the Roman Catholic children from every seminary of Protestants, even in those instances where none but the most miserable schools could be substituted in their room.[18]

The intensification of Catholic hostility to non-Catholic schools which took place about 1820, was not peculiar to the schools of the Association. Nevertheless, Catholics did attend these schools and many others like them, but it was a forced attendance embarrassing the Catholic clergy and causing much heart-burning to anxious parents. Such a situation could not last.

The Association, while perhaps not actively engaged in proselytism, nevertheless gave certain ground for believing that its indirect interest in the education of Catholics was not altogether altruistic. The times were not yet ripe for this. The printing of the New Testament in Irish was obviously directed at Catholics.[19] There were constant references in annual sermons and reports that 'until a great moral and religious change shall have taken place in this country' the union with England was in danger. These references left little doubt as to the Association's real attitude to Catholics. The Catholics on their part were not slow to realise this either, and the failure of the Association to revive the intentions of the 1537 Act was obvious to all, long before the commissioners in 1825 pronounced their schools to be at once too few in number and too Protestant in character to become generally available for the education of Roman Catholic children.[20] Sir Thomas Wyse saw in the schools of the Association, a milder form of the same spirit which led to the complete failure of the Charter Schools:

> There was no exclusion: Catholics were admitted as Catholics: no renunciation of their faith was required, but care was taken there should be Protestant patrons, Protestant teachers, Protestant versions of the Scriptures, and Protestant text books; Protestantism in every shape the moment they crossed the threshold.[21]

The Society for promoting the Education of the Poor of Ireland (the Kildare Place Society) was first inaugurated at a meeting held in Dublin on 2nd December 1811.[22] Among education societies the Kildare Place Society was to become, in point of educational work and scope of operation, the most progressive and important. With their liberal principles which were, to date, the most likely to be accepted by the Catholics without offending others, the Kildare Place Society could confidently hope that, in time, it would become truly national and act as a basis for uniting in a common purpose all classes of Irishmen.

However, the principle of undenominational religious teaching was in essence repugnant to Catholic teaching. Under ideal conditions it would exercise no appeal for them. But conditions were far from ideal. With sufficient safeguards and opportunities for separate religious instruction, and particularly if free from all suspicion, this vital, controversial issue might have resulted in an acceptable *modus operandi*. But during the formative years of the Society, from 1812 to 1817 or 1818, the cumulative effect of the wave of religious zeal for the conversion of the Irish Catholics already noted, made this section of the community suspicious of all educational efforts which included Bible reading as an essential for participation.

The people involved in the setting up of the Kildare Place Society were convinced of the necessity to teach the great truths of Christianity to the underprivileged: a purely secular education was unthinkable. We have also to take into consideration that in the world of Br. Rice's time 'it was unthinkable that the sons of the poor should be taught to read, much less to write or to cipher. Indeed the capitalist world in which he lived demanded that under no circumstances should the labouring man's son receive even the most elementary education'.[23]

On returning from Rome in 1817, Dr. Murray brought with him copies of the Rule and Papal Brief of Approbation of the Institute of the Christian Schools, founded in France in 1680 by St John Baptist de la Salle. Dr. Murray presented these to Br. Rice and urged him to study them carefully, requesting him to petition the Holy See for the necessary confirmation. The De la Salle Rule was very helpful and when all was in readiness, Br. Rice sent his proposed Rule and Constitution to Rome for approval. Br. Rice's petition was accompanied by letters of commendation from his Grace, the Archbishop of Dublin, Dr. Troy, Dr. Murray and other prelates.[24]

Within the unusually short time of two years, the Apostolic Brief, "Ad Pastoralis Dignitatis Fastigium", was issued by Pope Pius VII on 5th September, 1820. This gave formal approval to the Rules and constitution of the new Congregation and brought about great changes in its government. All the houses became united under a superior-general, an office which was first held by Edmund Ignatius Rice in 1822 after the deliberations of the General Chapter. Funds and administration were, in like manner, centralised and one novitiate was set up for all aspirants.

The speedy issue of the brief was in no small measure due to the anxiety of Pope Pius VII on the whole question of Bible Societies in Ireland. Through Cardinal Fontana, he addressed a letter on the topic to the Irish hierarchy on 18th September, 1818[25] urging upon them the importance of establishing Catholic schools in their dioceses. The society set up by Edmund Rice must have seemed to the Pope, a direct answer to his anxieties. "The personnel who were prepared to make self-sacrifice and forego any remuneration for their services were particularly suited to the age."[26]

Increased demands for new foundations were the direct result. At the time of the Brief there were 9 houses, 35 Brothers and close on 4,000 pupils in the various schools. Papal approval now brought with it certain privileges, as well as obligations.

In addition to the improved status of Br. Rice's congregation, as a result of papal approval, several other factors were operating at the time, about 1822, to bring the work of the Brothers more firmly before the public. Since 1820 the Catholic opposition to proselytism stiffened considerably and their demands for some share in the public funds for education grew all the louder as it became more unified. The form of education most repugnant to Catholics was that provided by the various Bible Societies. The schools of the Brothers and Nuns, being free, did help to counter the activity of these organisations as, for example, when the Brothers opened two houses in County Clare for that purpose, in Ennistymon in 1824 and in Ennis in 1827.[27] Brother Rice's schools in various parts of County Waterford forestalled the Bible schools, but attempts were made.[28] In Dublin, in the Archbishop's parish there were no fewer than 36 Protestant free schools attended by upwards of 1,000 Catholic children.[29] To counteract this, Br. Rice opened a temporary school in Jervis Street in 1828 and this was subsequently transferred to North Richmond Street, where the foundation stone was laid by Daniel O'Connell amid great rejoicing. The school bears his name to this day. The big schools run by the religious orders, were in enrolment the equivalent of 10 or 12 smaller schools, and it was through the large town school that the religious orders did their most effective work for Catholics.

The failure of the Kildare Place Society to hold the approval of Catholics was another circumstance which brought into greater prominence the schools of the religious orders and acted as a spur towards the setting up of increasing numbers of schools by Catholics themselves. The Kildare Place Society, which at the commencement of its labours in 1811, seemed likely to give satisfaction and which included some prominent Catholics in its Committee, gradually lost Catholic approval through its support of proselytising societies. After 1820, it ceased to be an effective organisation for the education of the poor and very large numbers of Catholic children were withdrawn from its schools.

Writing on the *First Report* (1825) of the Commissioners of Irish

Education Inquiry, another Protestant observer said, with regard to the Brothers' schools in Cork and Limerick – the two biggest in the country at the time – that they

> commenced upon the liberal foundation of partnership without principle and ended in the natural result of religion without the Bible.[30]

Between the years 1820 and 1824, the education question reached its climax. On the Catholic side two factors emerged. The fundamental opposition to the Bible Societies and the developed opposition to the Kildare Place Society, a Government sponsored and financed organisation, hardened. It was now realised by the Catholics that no system of Education except their own could be trusted. In all probability they realised this all along but pressing poverty gave little choice. After 1820, they set up more schools of their own and called for a commission of inquiry with a view to obtaining some measure of financial assistance. Their action not only showed the Government that there was an ever increasing number of Catholic schools, but also brought out more clearly the failure of such schemes as the Kildare Place Society. In retrospect, the position of the Catholics about 1820, has all the appearance of a well planned manoeuvre; in reality they were activated mainly by the dangers to the religious beliefs of the Catholic children in non-Catholic schools. Official quarters saw such ultra Catholic schools as those established by religious orders, coupled with an increasing number of smaller, common schools where official policy held no writ, as very dangerous. However, the gradual failure of schemes, both private and public, to entice Catholics into schools more in keeping with ascendancy views was the crunch factor. Between official fears of losing every vestige of control and Catholic financial inability to remain completely independent lay the seeds of compromise.

However, the schools of the Brothers and Nuns spearheaded the attack on town-education without further help from the state. The work of the Commission of 1824, further highlighted the labours of the Christian Brothers. The Commissioners visited the principal schools established by Br. Rice and left on record the good impression made on them as well as an account of the curriculum followed in the Hanover Street East School, Dublin –

> And we are informed that the same system is adopted in all the others.[31]

As a by-product of the Commission many influential people came over from England to assess the educational situation for themselves. Many of these people visited the Brothers schools[32] and left on record the favourable impressions made upon them.

Within two years of the Commissioners' *First Report* (1825) the Christian Brothers had opened houses in Preston, Manchester and Soho, London[33] and a further house in Jervis Street.

Considering all the circumstances of the time, it is understandable that a religious society such as Mr. Rice's should arouse a good deal of comment both friendly and hostile. To many Protestants of the period, religious orders or societies were suspect and a century of persecution had left them with no very clear ideas as to what a full-blooded Catholic education meant. When Br. Rice completed the school in North Richmond St. after having money collected for it in England and having added one thousand pounds of his own money, he found it difficult to get the water supply of the city connected to the school. The Protestant City Corporation refused his requests. Br. Rice, with the help of a water diviner, found a plentiful supply thirty feet below the foundations of the school. Before the year 1832 had passed, he had provided splendid schools for over 600 boys, many of whom had been unwilling victims of the education provided in the fifteen proselytising boys schools in the parish.[34] The Rev. R. H. Hyland in his *History of Waterford* (1824), gives a liberal Protestant view of the work of Mr. Rice's society:

> Amongst a distressed and unemployed population whose religious opinions militate against the system of education offered by their Protestant brethren, these schools (of Edmund Rice) have been of incalculable benefit; they have also impressed upon the lower classes a character which hitherto was unknown to them . . . Mr. Rice was a monk and though unquestionably conscientious and munificent in the founding of his school he unhappily rendered their ecclesiastical character so very important that they are in the broadest manner, in both spirit and design Roman Catholic.[35]

Mr. Hyland gives no clues as to what kind of education he expected Mr. Rice to provide for the Catholic children of Waterford. Some considered the system of education followed by the Brothers as being "the most intolerant and mischievous" ever devised.[36] But these were a minority. Most of those capable of giving an unprejudiced opinion left the question of religious instruction as a matter for Catholics themselves and confined their comments to the secular instruction given and the great improvement in the conduct of the poor boys. The majority of those who spoke and wrote in favour of the Brothers, when certain clauses in the proposed Emancipation Bill threatened them with extinction, were of this latter class. Sir John Newport, parliamentary representative for Waterford, wrote to Lamb (later Lord Melbourne) asking him to use his influence with the Duke of Devonshire on behalf of Mr. Rice's Institute.[37]

Of the 15 establishments that comprised Edmund Rice's Institute in the year 1838, most of them were founded by local clergymen and others who were interested in the education of poor boys. Of the two founded, personally by him, that in North Richmond Street, Dublin was probably his greatest achievement.[38]

Within a few decades of their founding, the schools of the Christian Brothers had reached a position of remarkable promise and influence. They found favour with Catholic and Protestant alike; bishops and priests, Members of Parliament, influential gentlemen from many walks of life, and not least the Commissioners of Education spoke well of them. What was the reason for their success? What did they teach, how did they teach it and what manner of man was Edmund Rice who inspired others and brought about an educational revolution? Before these questions are answered it is well to note that the success of the Brothers' schools was in the first place due to the singleness of purpose which inspired all the teachers: a religious zeal for the education of the children in the only way really acceptable. The schools were successful because they ignored all compromise and were essentially Catholic. Much more than this was needed for success but they did have a common foundation which ensured co-operation in essentials and made for greater cohesion in particulars.

From a Christian point of view, the most important aspect of education is the spiritual, which embraces the proper understanding of man's relationship with God and the expression given to that relationship through worship and obedience in association with His Church. Religious instruction is but a means to this end. In the schools of the Christian Brothers' religious instruction, essentially factual, was coupled with frequent opportunity for the practical development of the spiritual life. Neither was religion cut off from the daily routine, as happened with the later National Board schools, but formed the basis of the school atmosphere, being the motivating force of all activity. The pupils caught something of this religious spirit from their teachers, all of whom had sacrificed worldly opportunity with this end in view. There was nothing artificial or forced about the process and in due course the refining influence of this religious atmosphere made itself felt among the neglected children who crowded the classrooms.

Almost a century later the *Freeman's Journal* asserted:

> Down through the dark days of persecution, these Brothers with a price on their heads, kept alive amongst the young, the love of God and devotion to their country.[39]

For a historian, Edmund Rice was an important providential instrument to re-forge an ancient Celtic people. He gave hope to the 'Martyr Nation' at the cultural crossroads of its history. For a nineteenth century Catholic, his nationality was contained in his nation's religious history. The Irish urban poor never abandoned their ancient faith but the renewed hostility of evangelism was then a new powerful force. Keeping a very low profile, Br. Rice with his gifted band of followers reacted against the enormous amount of anti-Irish prejudice which permeated nineteenth century literature and newspapers. The timid Catholic hierarchy was his great supporter in his new sphere of education.

There was no compromise in his approach. For the Catholic Church, all other efforts to teach the people had become a giant impious conspiracy to destroy the faith
> . . ., while the English mind secularised the spiritual and sacred, the Irish mind saw all in terms of Heaven and Hell.[40]

Bishop Russell of Waterford speaking on the withdrawal of the Christian Brothers from Clonmel, summed up neatly the contribution of Edmund Rice:

> They are the men who passed on the faith, the men who helped people up when they were down, and helped instil in young people a sense of hope. And we hope that the teachers of today can find the strength to overcome the present sense of hopelessness.[41]

A Timely Restorer of Faith and Hope in Ireland

References

1. Rushe, D., *Edmund Rice The Man and His Times*, (1981),
2. *Third Report* (Education of the Lower Classes), 15, H.C.1826-27 (13) xiii
3. Endowed Schools (Ireland) Commission 1854-58, ii, 363
4. *Third Report* 116 seqq., H.C. 1826-27 (13) xiii
5. Registry of Deeds Dublin, 715, 145, 489080 as in Fitzpatrick, op.cit, 126
6. 31 George III, c.32
7. Normoyle, M. C., *A Tree Is Planted*, Chapter 6 and P. 158
8. *The Waterford Mirror*, January 1809, cited by Fitzpatrick, Edmund Rice, 162
9. Normoyle, *op.cit.*, Chapter 7
10. Hughes, P., *The Catholic Question: 1688-1820*, 250
11. Coolahan, J., *Irish Education: History and Structure*, 9
12. Bowen, D., *The Protestant Crusade in Ireland 1800-70*, 96 seqq
13. *Thirteenth Report* (English Schools of Private Foundation in Ireland), 324, H. C. 1813-14 (47) v
14. *First Report*, 32, H.C.1825 (400) xii
15. *Thirteenth Report*, 324,H.C. 1813-14 (47) v. The Parochial Schoolmasters (Scotland) Act of 1803 prescribed salaries ranging from £16 to £22 per annum
16. *First Report*, Ibid.
17. *First Report*, Ibid.
18. *Report of the Association for Discountenancing Vice . . .*, (1826), 22
19. *General Report of the Association . . .*, (1826), Appendix I, xxv
20. *First Report*, 35, H. C. (1825) 400, xiii. 37
21. Wyse, Winifred M., *Notes on Education Reform in Ireland during the first half of the nineteenth century: compiled from Speeches etc. contained in the unpublished memoirs of the Right Honourable Sir Thomas Wyse*, 5
22. Lynch, Michael A., *The Kildare Place Society 1811-1870* (unpublished M.A. Thesis, UCC, 1958)
23. Fitzpatrick, J. D., 'Zeal for spreading the glory of God', in Christian Brothers: *Educational Record* (1963), 17
24. Fitzpatrick, *op.cit.*, 181
25. Fitzpatrick, *op.cit.*, 182-185
26. Atkinson, N., *Irish Education* (1969), 74
27. *Educational Record*, (1895), 106
28. *Waterford Morning Register*, 2 November, 1824
29. *Fourth Report* (1831) of the Education Society for the Instruction of the Poor. This was a Catholic Society.
30. *Practical Observations upon the views and tendency of the First Report of the Commissioners of Irish Education Inquiry*, 32-33
31. *First Report*, 85, H.C. (1825), 5400, xii
32. *Educational Record*, (1894), 467 seqq
33. *Ibid.*
34 Fitzpatrick, *art. cit.*, 24
35 Hyland, R. H. *History of Waterford* (1824), cited in Fitzpatrick, *op. cit.*, 261
36. *Practical Observations . . . of the First Report . . .*, 33
37. Archives Rome; Rice's reply to Newport. The original of Mr. Rice's letter is in the PRO Dublin
38. Fitzpatrick, *art. cit.*, 22
39. *Freeman's Journal*, 13 November, 1916
40. O'Farrell, P., *Ireland's English Question* (1972), 4
41. *The Nationanlist*, Saturday, 10 July, 1993

A Man Raised Up

Bibliography

Archives Rome; Rice's reply to Newport. The original of Mr. Rice's letter is in the PRO Dublin

Atkinson, N., *Irish Education* (1969), 74

Bowen, D., *The Protestant Crusade in Ireland 1800-70* (Dublin, 1978)

Christian Brothers, *Educational Record*, (1887-ongoing),

Coolahan, J. *Irish Education: History and Structure* (Dublin, 1981).

Endowed Schools (Ireland) Commision 1854-58, ii, 363

First Report of the Commissioners of Inquiry. 1825 (400) xii.1.

Fitzpatrick, J. D., *Edmund Rice* (Dublin, 1945).

Fourth Report (1831) of the Education Society for the Instruction of the poor. This was a Catholic Society.

Freeman's Journal, 13 November, 1916

General Report of the Association . . ., (1820), Appendix I,xxv

Hughes, P., *The Catholic Question: 1688-1829. A Study in Political History* (London 1929)

Hyland, R. H. *History of Waterford* (1924), cited in Fitzpatrick, *op.cit.*, 261

Lynch, Michael A., *The Kildare Place Society 1811-1870* (unpublished thesis, U.C.C 1958)

Normoyle, M. C., *A Tree is Planted*, (2nd Edition, 1976), Private Circulation.

O'Farrell, P., *Ireland's English Question* (New York, 1972).

Registry of Deeds, Dublin, 715, 145.

Report of the Association for Discountenacing Vice . . ., (1826), 22

Reports of the Commissioners of the Board of Education in Ireland, persuant to 46 George III, c.122.

Rushe, D. *Edmund Rice: The Man and his Times*, (1981), p.145.

Edmund Rice and Saint Teresa of Avila

Seán E. Ó Cearbhaill, CFC

W HEN EDMUND RICE was born in Co. Kilkenny, Ireland, the decrees of the Council of Trent were beginning to influence the Catholic Church in Ireland. "The religious life of the people," says Patrick Corish, "was (being) rooted in the catechesis of the Counter-Reformation" (Corish 131). Things were changing, especially in the towns. The Confraternity of Christian Doctrine, one of the very successful instruments of the Tridentine Reform, had become quite popular throughout Ireland, particularly in certain rural areas and in the towns. Through the Confraternity and its libraries the spiritual classics of the Counter-Reformation, in translation from various European languages, were becoming popular. Old values were being re-discovered through these writings and new life was resulting in the growth of the Spirit in many people. A whole fresh flowering of consecrated life followed in the beginning of the nineteenth century. Today, the influence of another Church Council, Vatican II, is seeping through to the People of God and, in spite of some upheaval and some evident disorganisation, the receding waters of the high tide of its newness has laid bare some old treasures and some forgotten influences. The attempts at renewal of religious life have opened old mines and a realisation has been born in some congregations that these old mines could be productive of new riches and new life in the spirit, for these congregations. In the congregations of the Presentation Brothers and the Irish Christian Brothers devotion to Saint Teresa of Avila is just one such area for exploration.

There was always a tradition, or rather a memory, in the Congregation of the Irish Christian Brothers that Edmund Rice, their Founder, was very devoted to St. Teresa of Avila. It was also believed that some of the early Brothers and some aspects of the very life of the Congregation in the early days were influenced by this great doctor of the Church. This ancient tradition was like a map, a family heirloom, that people believed existed but were not sure where it was or what it signified.

Brother Stephen Carroll (born 1813) entered the Christian Brothers in 1835. He knew Edmund Rice personally and has left it on record in 1888 that the Founder "was very devout to

115

St.Teresa and fond of reading her works" (Normoyle, *Memories* 40). He reports a conversation he had with Edmund Rice: "I heard him say he took particular notice of that saying of hers where she described the poverty she experienced in one of her foundations, where she says she had not so much fire in the house as she would roast a sprat on." Certainly Edmund Rice's Rule of 1832 shows a similar desire to be poor as Christ was: "No Brother shall have anything in propriety; all things shall be in common in each house" (1832 Rule 26). Brother Alphonsus Collins (born 1841) also left it in writing that Edmund Rice was "exceedingly devout" to St.Teresa. He says that her feast day was "kept a festive day with the old Brothers" (*Memories* 63). Brother Collins refers to an early confrere of Edmund Rice, Brother Austin Grace: "There was one saint in particular, Brother Grace used to tell us, in whom the Founder had great confidence and to whom he practised a special devotion and that was Saint Teresa. He had great faith in her intercession." (*Memories* 63). Continuing, Brother Collins adds: "It is to be noted that Saint Teresa has been a favourite with our people, and she and Saint Brigid are the two female saints with whose names they are familiar. A number of Irish girls are called after them". Brother Regis Hughes (born 1841) wrote that Edmund Rice "was a great admirer of Saint Teresa and very much resembled her in the practical, sensible view she took of everything" (*Memories* 146). A niece of Brother John Wiseman (born 1795), one of the contemporaries of Edmund Rice, wrote in 1912 that her uncle "was devout to the Blessed Virgin, to Saint Joseph and to Saint Teresa". "This devotion," she said "was promoted under Brother Rice" (*Memories* 329).

Brother Dominic Burke, in his account of the early days of the Christian Brothers tells us concerning Edmund Rice: "He was remarkably devout to Saint Teresa; her feast day was always one of special devotion with him, and from him all his early companions took up this devotion. He kept a picture of the saint in his room, and often would he be seen pressing his lips to it. His devotion to this great saint became more remarkable as life drew to its close; but, as might be expected, his devotion to the Holy Mother of God was most intense" (*History of the Institute* 1.392).

Brother Mark McCarthy, in his biography of Edmund Rice published in 1926, also refers to the Founder's devotion to St. Teresa: "After the Holy Scriptures, no spiritual book attracted

him so much as the writings of Saint Teresa. He always observed
her feast day with much solemnity, and had it noted with many
others as a day of special devotion for the Brothers" (*McCarthy*
416). Brother David Fitzpatrick, in his work on Edmund Rice,
which was published in 1945, also refers to Edmund Rice's
devotion to St.Teresa: "His sentiments and aspirations were in
complete accord with those of his great exemplar, St.Teresa . . .
In Br. Rice's favourite volumes, The Bible, Butler's Feasts and
Fasts, and the works of St.Teresa, penance is ranked equally
with prayer and alms-deeds in the devout life" (*Fitzpatrick* 290/1).
And again: "Another of his patrons was St.Teresa of Avila whose
picture he kept in his room and whose feast day he observed
with special devotion" (*Fitzpatrick* 289). Incidentally, there is a
copy of an old engraving of St. Teresa in the present museum in
Mount Sion. This writer recalls pictures of St.Teresa in some of the
bedrooms in Mount Sion in the 1940's. There was also a tradition
in Mount Sion that the fires in the house were first lit and cloaks
were first worn on the Feast of St.Teresa.

There is evidence that Edmund Rice was familiar with many
of the spiritual classics of the Counter-Reformation. He was
well acquainted with the works of St. Ignatius of Loyola and
of St. Francis de Sales (1832 Rule 29). He had a special love for
Scupoli's *Spiritual Combat*. Scupoli was a Theatine and his book
was as important to the Theatines as was *The Spiritual Exercises*
to the Jesuits. A Kempis and Scupoli were quite popular at the
time. "The reverence which Saint Ignatius of Loyola had for
the *Imitation of Christ* was matched by that of Saint Francis
de Sales for the *Spiritual Combat*" (*O'Toole* 1.87). "Scupoli's
Spiritual Combat" says O'Toole "had been the *vade-mecum* of
Saint Francis de Sales for over twenty years; it had been his
primer in the school of holiness." "For Edmund Rice too," he
continues "this dear book, so clear and so practical in its teaching
was to become a prolific source of spiritual blessings" (*O'Toole*
1.87). Edmund Rice was close to the Jesuits in Waterford City and
devoted to Saint Ignatius. Eventually, however, as he progressed
in the ways of the spirit, says O'Toole, "Saint Teresa, her life and
her writings, was to become the major influence on his spiritual
life" (*O'Toole* 1.88). Finally, continues O'Toole, "it could be said
that his favourite books were the Bible and the works of Saint
Teresa".

What was the particular attraction of the great saint of Avila for Edmund Rice? It is possible that he had devotion to her from quite an early period in his life. Saint Teresa was a popular saint in Ireland in the seventeenth and eighteenth centuries, presumably because of the Irish links with Spain. Moreover, Kilkenny, which was his native county, had been a Carmelite mission since the thirteenth century. The White Friar Abbey of the Holy Saviour at Knocktopher (a few miles from where Edmund Rice was born) was founded in 1356 and was one of the earliest foundations by the so-called "Mitigated Carmelites" (*O'Toole* 1.271). Knocktopher was once the head house of the Order in Ireland (Ó Fearghaíl 212). The Irish Catholic exiles who joined the Carmelites of the Teresian Reform in Spain brought back her spirit to their own country. They certainly had introduced the Reform to Ireland by 1625 and by 1683 they had an Irish Province. Edmund Rice could have met them while he was a high school student in Kilkenny for they had a monastery there. Besides, from 1795-1800, the Parish Priest in Callan (Edmund's native parish) was Father Milea, a Carmelite. Could it have been that Edmund Rice spoke to Father Milea in 1793 or 1794 when he came to consult the local bishop about founding his Brotherhood? O'Toole speculates that Edmund Rice's knowledge of Teresa and her teaching probably came from his reading of the Life. Butler's *Lives of the Saints* was a popular compendium in family libraries in Ireland. Published first in 1780 it contained a comprehensive account of Saint Teresa and of her life and works. In 1794 an abridged version of Butler's biography of Teresa was edited by Rev. John Milner and published in Ireland by subscription. By 1795, the *Life of Holy Mother, Saint Teresa* was being offered to the general public on a list of popular spiritual books on sale from the Dublin publishers, Meighan and Cross (*O'Toole* 1.272). It is interesting to note here what Abbot Butler had written in his Lives of the Saints for the 15th of October, the Feast of Saint Teresa:

> The humble relation which Saint Teresa has left of her own life in obedience to her confessors is the delight of devout persons, not on account of the revelations and visions there recorded, but because in it are laid down the most perfect maxims by which a soul is conducted in the path of obedience, humility

and self-denial, and especially of prayer and an interior life. (Quoted in *O'Toole* 1.272).

The rules of most religious orders or congregations, including even the Benedictine and Jesuit Rules are generally, as has been said, "a mosaic of borrowings". Edmund Rice, when he founded his first Brotherhood also borrowed freely. In 1802 he took the Rule of the Presentation Sisters as a suitable rule to hand. In that rule the Sisters mentioned "Mary, ever Virgin and Mother of God" as their principal patroness. Then followed a list of sixteen saints towards whom the members were to have special devotion. In his adaptation of the Presentation Rule for his own Brothers, Edmund Rice kept this list of Our Lady and the sixteen other saints. But he added three further saints to the list; Saint John the Baptist, Saint Ignatius of Loyola and Saint Teresa (*O'Toole* 1,165). Edmund Rice owed a great debt to the Jesuits. They were his personal friends and had helped him in many ways. He took the name Brother Ignatius as his new name in religion. And yet, as O'Toole points out, he must have had a very special interest in Saint Teresa.

From my recent reading of the works of Saint Teresa, I am slowly being convinced that the influence of the Saint of Avila on his spirituality and on that of the early Brothers was much greater than we ever realised. O'Toole says that "the spirit of prayer which he subsequently cultivated was certainly Teresian in character" (*O'Toole* 1.272). Certainly this seems verified, for example, by the substituton which Edmund Rice made in Chapter VI of the Presentation Sisters' Rule. The section was "On Enclosure." Realising that strict enclosure would not suit his own busy life nor the lives of the Brothers working in so many ways for the poverty-stricken families they served, he replaced the directions for canonical enclosure with a "spiritual enclosure" that was certainly Teresian: "The religious Brothers of this pious institute should propose to themselves to aspire to one of the most essential qualities of religious perfection, viz., an entire detachment from creatures and a holy union with God."

From a preliminary study there are certainly elements in Edmund Rice's way of going to God that harmonise with well-known elements in Teresa's spirituality. His ideas on prayer are very much her ideas. He, a widower, would understand the concept of a spousal relationship with Christ. Like Teresa, Edmund Rice had a remarkable love for the Church and a great concern for its interests. Like Teresa, he too suffered calumny and humiliation in its service. Then again, the Presence of God was a living and constant awareness in his life as it was with Teresa. In the question of his correspondence there was also an affinity between them. Professor A. Peers points out that "Saint Teresa's correspondence, in the main, was concerned not with spiritual matters but with business." "Yet" he continues "it is the real Teresa, not the saint in the niches, that appears in these letters" (*O'Toole* II.53). The letters of Edmund Rice are also, for the most part, business letters. And he too, like Teresa, could in the midst of discussing business, turn aside to speak of the meaning of a life lived for God. A typical example of this is the oft-quoted letter of Edmund Rice to his business friend, Bryan Bolger, 10 August 1810 (Normoyle, *Companion* 7):

> I am sorry to be giving you so much trouble; perhaps it may come in my way to do as much for you; however I hope God will supply our inability in this way . . . How many of our actions are lost for want of applying them to this end, and were we to know the merit and value of only going from one street to another to serve a neighbour for the love of God, we should prize it more than gold or silver.

In the final paragraph of the letter he returns to the business in hand and ends with: "The Will of God be done in this and in everything we undertake."

In his book *Spiritual Pilgrim* John Welch O.Carm. summarises Teresa's message: "God calls us into life and into the fullness of our personhood. Centering our life in God does not rob us of our personality but guarantees it" (*Welch* 1). This paper is but the beginning of a search. I hope to make it the initiation of a study of how much Saint Teresa influenced the spiritual growth of Edmund Rice. On 27 September 1970 she was proclaimed, along with Saint Catherine of Siena, Doctor of the Church, by Pope Paul VI. Pope Pius X had said of her: "So great has been her influence that it is second only to that of the greatest Fathers and Doctors of the Church, if indeed it is second to them" (*Venard* xii).

At this stage I think it would be useful to compare some of the

Part of the original Mount Sion

Reconstruction of Founder's room. The picture on the wall is that of St. Teresa.

statements and ideas found in the writings of Edmund Rice with similar ideas and statements from the works of Saint Teresa:

The Will of God
Saint Teresa: "But never, not even in its first stirrings does the will turn from its desire that God's Will be done in it" (*Spiritual Test* 65.9).
Edmund Rice: "I must confess that I am not very desirous of having them permanently settled in that parish . . . May the Will of God be done in it"
(E. Rice to B. Bolger, 20/12/1813)

The Vanity of the World
Saint Teresa: "I began to understand the truth I knew in childhood (the nothingness of all things, the vanity of the world, and how it would soon come to an end)" (*Life* 3.5)
Edmund Rice: "The world and everything in it is continually changing which proves to us that there is nothing permanent under the sun, and that perfect happiness is not to be expected but in another world"
(E. Rice to Mother Knowd, 2 Nov. 1813).

God's Time
Saint Teresa: "Once again it is very important for the spirit not to ascend unless the Lord raise it up" (*Life* 12.7).
Edmund Rice: "But we must wait for God's Time"
(E. Rice to Mother M. Wall, 20 Feb. 1839).

Recollection
Saint Teresa: "this prayer is called 'recollection' because the soul collects its faculties together and enters within itself to be with its God" (*Way of Perfection* 28.4).
Edmund Rice: " . . . Thus will they preserve the spirit of holy disengagement. They shall always manifest a love of holy retirement and strictly observe it as far as is compatible with their state; they shall seek by holy recollection and prayer to draw down this spirit from God" (Adaptation for Rule of 1832 2.13).

The Presence of God
Saint Teresa: "It used to happen, when I represented Christ within me in order to place myself in his Presence or even while reading, that a feeling of the Presence of God would come upon me

unexpectedly, so that I could in no way doubt He was within me or I totally immersed in him" (*Life* 10.1).

Edmund Rice: "On entering into their cells, if the Brothers intend to remain there for any considerable time, they shall place themselves on their knees, for the space of a Hail Mary or thereabouts, to adore God present; also on their entering the community room at the hours of recreation: and in the study-room immediately before study" (1832 Rule 3.5)

Nature

Saint Teresa: "Those who follow this path of non-discursive reflection will find that a book can be of help for recollecting oneself quickly. It helped me also to look at fields, or water, or flowers. In these things I found a remembrance of the Creator" (*Life* 9.5).

Edmund Rice: "He loved to sit at his window, as an old man, and look at the fields, and the flowers and the cattle" (*History of the Institute* 1.47).

Patience

Saint Teresa: "His Majesty gave me a great favour from the Lord, for this patience was clearly seen to come from Him . . . I kept these words of Job very habitually in my mind and recited them: 'since we receive good things from the hand of the Lord, why do we not suffer the evil things? This it seems gave me strength" (*Life* 5.8).

Edmund Rice: "Although our trial ended on this day week no decision has yet taken place . . . It is a painful anxiety, but to some of us it is not so much as one may imagine. 'The Lord gave and the Lord taketh away, so blessed be His name for ever and ever.' This should be all our motto . . ." (E. Rice to P. Corbett, 3/7/1835).

Service

Saint Teresa: "While reflecting on the friendship with Our Lord . . . The Lord told me that from now on I should try hard, that I was going to have to serve Him more than I did up to this point" (*Spiritual Testimonies* 37).

Edmund Rice: "O God, did we even now rightly begin to serve you, your loving heart would take us again into your fond embrace" (*History of the Institute* 1.393).

Creatures
Saint Teresa: "The soul is left with greater contempt for the world than before because it sees that nothing in the world was any help to it in that torment, and it is much more detached from creatures because it now sees that only the Creator can console and satisfy it" (*Interior Castle* VI.10).
Edmund Rice: "It is a poor thing, I must own, to be expecting the reward of labour from creatures who frequently are forgetful and ungrateful for favours done them, but let us do ever so little for God we will be sure he will never forget it, nor let it pass unrewarded" (E. Rice to B. Bolger, 10/8/1810).

Detachment
Saint Teresa: "The soul detaches itself from everything so as to abide more in God" (*Life* 18.14).
Edmund Rice: "to view nothing but with the eyes of faith, to do nothing but with a view to God . . . Thus will they preserve the spirit of holy disengagement"
(1832 Rule 11.2).

Compassion
Saint Teresa: "It is good and necessary sometimes in loving to show . . . and to feel some of the trials and sicknesses of the Sisters, even though these may be small Little things can bring much distress to persons who have sensitive natures" (*Way of Perfection* 7.5).
Edmund Rice: "Maybe you'd have the goodness to apologise for me with our Sisters in James's Street. I neither took my leave, nor did I see them for near a week before I left Dublin. Tell them the only excuse I have to make for my ingratitude is to acknowledge it. Tell them that for the last days I was a good deal occupied and, what was worse, that my spirits were for the most part as low as ditch water"
(E. Rice to Mother Biggar 20/12/1813).

The above quotations are but a cursory study of some indications that Edmund Rice was influenced by Saint Teresa. Her warm humanity and her practical single-minded pursuit of union with God seemed to have allied themselves with the spirit of Edmund Rice. This combination seems to have been assimilated by some of the early members of his Brotherhood. A letter from Brother

125

Myles Kelly to Edmund Rice when the latter was old, retired and broken in health captures some of that spirit:

> It is happy for you to have no care on you but to enjoy a dignified repose for the remainder of your days, increasing hourly in the love of God, and preparing to quit this exile and take possession of the heavenly Jerusalem (M. I. Kelly to E. Rice, 2/4/1841).

This is a spirit that seems to have faded with the changing historical circumstances of our story as a congregation. We, Christian Brothers, for many years back, have seen ourselves like other nineteenth century congregations as cast in an Ignatian mould. Maybe a study of Saint Teresa and of her system of working towards union with God would be fruitful in a rediscovery of our Founder. Who knows but that it would give us a basis for a new approach to our life and work as an apostolic congregation.

As I have already stated in this paper, the study of Saint Teresa and the parallel study of Edmund Rice and of his devotion to the Saint is a new area that has definite possibilities. It could hold the key to the knowledge of much of the inner life of this man. Teresa's writings and reform coincided with the Reform of Carmel and indirectly with the reform of many other forms of religious life. Maybe today it could initiate a particular approach to renewal and to new life in Edmund Rice's two congregations. We are all, at present, in the process of implementing the documents of the Second Vatican Council for the renewal of the Church. It is interesting that Edmund Rice's initiative for God came out of the flowing waters of another renewing process that followed on the results of a previous Church Council. The teachings of that Council helped God's people through a transitional period in the history of the Church and of the world at that particular time. Much of what happened then is also happening now. Their situation parallels many of the elements of our situation in the Church and in the world of today. Maybe some of their solutions and some of the great spirit of the founders and the foundresses of so many movements for God that came alive in those years may come again. For the two congregations of Edmund Rice there could be special benefits and blessings awaiting their return to the devotion to and the study of Saint Teresa of Avila.

Edmund Rice and Saint Teresa of Avila

Works Cited

Corish, Patrick. *The Irish Catholic Experience*. Dublin: Gill and MacMillan, 1985.

Doyle, E. B. ed., J. D. Burke. *The History of the Institute* 3 vols. Dublin: Christian Brothers, n.d.

Fitzpatrick, J. D. *Edmund Rice*. Dublin: M. H. Gill and Son, 1945.

McCarthy, W. M. *Edmund Ignatius Rice and the Christian Brothers*. Dublin: M. H. Gill and Son, 1926.

Normoyle, M. C. *A Companion to the Tree is Planted*. Dublin: Christian Brothers, 1977.

Memories of Edmund Rice. Dublin: Christian Brothers, 1979.

Ó Fearghaíl, Ferghus. *The Catholic Church in Co. Kilkenny 1600-1800*. in W. Nolan & K. Whelan, eds., Kilkenny: *History and Society*. Dublin: Geography Publications, 1990.

O'Toole, A. L. *A Spiritual Profile of Edmund Ignatius Rice*. 2 vols. Bristol: Burleigh Press, 1985.

Rodriguez, Otilio and Kieran Kavanaugh. Trans. *The Collected Works of Saint Teresa of Avila*. 2 vols. Washington: ICS Publications, 1980.

Rules and Constitutions of the Society of Religious Brothers. Dublin: Christian Brothers, 1832.

Venard, John, OCD. *The Interior Castle, Saint Teresa of Avila*. Sydney: E. J. Dwyer, 1989.

Welch, John. *Spiritual Pilgrims*. New York Paulist Press, 1982.

Dublin: Triumph and Failure

Frank S. Keane, CFC

The First Foundation

EDMUND RICE experienced his greatest triumph in Dublin: Papal approval of his institute can be directly, though not exclusively, ascribed to developments in the capital. His most painful disappointments were also experienced in Dublin. Can we say that the lack of co-operation between the Brothers and the Archbishop in successive projects represents failure?

At the time of Daniel Murray's consecration (1809) as bishop Dublin had 200,000 Catholics, served by just 100 priests[1]. In the closing quarter of the eighteenth century the city had just 48 Catholic schools with just 225 pupils.[2] Girls were catered for in just one school, the Presentation Convent at George's Hill, founded by Teresa Mulally. Father Bethage SJ had established two schools for boys.[3]

Stephen P. Curtis, in a speech made in 1845, a year after Edmund's, death, described both his vision and his methodology in bringing it to reality.

"What did he effect? What, I should rather ask, did he not effect in that pursuit to which every pulsation of his heart, every aspiration of his soul, was for so many years devoted – the education of the working classes; the amelioration of their condition . . . his expansive intellect, far from suffering itself to be engrossed with pecuniary speculations, took a wider range, dwelt for years on the condition of his Catholic fellow countrymen, and seeing them in a state only one degree superior to that from which they had of late emerged, resolved that not with him, at least would rest the fault should they remain in it much longer. Unenlightened they were, and without a prospect of enlightenment! Schools they had none, save those establishments throughout the country where proselytism had made its lair . . . Everything was adverse; everywhere was difficulty; but in Edmund Rice there was a happy combination of those noble qualities, ardour, endurance, foresight, perseverance, which eminently fitted him for gigantic actions, and made him less consider the magnitude of the obstacles than the means of overcoming them . . ."[4]

Proselytism was rampant in Dublin. Thousands of Catholic boys and girls were lured into schools and taught trades, but at the cost of losing their religion. Bishop Murray saw in the Brothers' schools a system to counteract the proselytiser. Edmund realised that he could do something for the Catholic boys of Dublin. At the same time he appreciated the fact that foundations in Dublin would hasten the realisation of his dream of having schools in "Most parts of the kingdom".[5] An enormous challenge faced him. Pragmatically he did not just consider the problems; he undertook means to overcome them. To face such a task one needed those qualities described by Curtis: ardour, endurance, foresight, perseverance. In Dublin Edmund needed them. Events prove that he had them in abundance.

Edmund's constant prayer, "May God's will be done", shows how he accepted both successes and failures, as representing for him God's will. He recommended to the Brothers "to view nothing but with the eyes of faith".[6] His own faith was tested, and not found wanting.

Writing to Rome a decade later Edmund described the obstacle of the Bible, proselytising, schools: "some thousands of pounds are annually given, and for the present year £32,000 or so given, by the British Parliament to the Bible School Societies of this Kingdom";[7] Catholic schools get no state aid because their "teachers use the Catholic Bible quite differently and in a diametrically opposite sense to that used by the Bible schools."[8] He could legitimately assert that his schools were successful: "They (the Brothers) could appeal to the thousands who now crowd their schools, notwithstanding the bribes held to them, to induce them to the various Bible proselytising Schools with which this Country swarms."[9]

No documents have survived indicating who took the initiative in making a foundation in Dublin. But we can be certain that the move to Dublin, just ten years since the first school was opened in the stable in New Street, Waterford, did not come about without serious examination of the situation, and a confidence of success. John Wyse Power when speaking of Edmund relates: "It was said that he never took any step of importance until assured of the Divine guidance, but that when once resolved upon a course of action he could not be turned aside from his object."[10] In 1810, writing to Archbishop Thomas Bray of Cashel and Emly, Edmund said, "I trust in the goodness of God that it (Brothers'

Institute) will spread before long in most parts of the Kingdom."[11] Characteristically he added, "May God give you grace to see this effected."[12] Edmund saw the need for Catholic schools in Ireland and England. An overriding consideration was to attract sufficient vocations to ensure that Brothers were available to staff the schools.

When Edmund Rice sent Brother Thomas John-Baptist Grosvenor to Dublin in 1812[13] he sacrificed his greatest friend and most accomplished associate. In 1813 Edmund resigned all authority over Grosvenor and his unidentified companion, to the Archbishop, agreeing to support both from resources in Waterford.[14] With two Brothers under his jurisdiction, the Archbishop became 'interested' in making a permanent establishment.[15] All looked well; the committee established a school and residence at the junction of East Hanover and Lime Streets.[16] The first school at Sir John Rogerson's Quay[17] and the temporary residence at Moira (now Albert Place)[18] were vacated. However, very quickly confidence was shaken when Bishop John Power of Waterford, who, in 1812, reluctantly agreed to sending the two Brothers to Dublin,[19] seeing decreasing returns from investments, voiced his objection, to money, rightly intended for the schools in Waterford, being spent in Dublin.[20]

The pioneering years of the Dublin school were not without worries. The actions of one member of the school committee, Mr. Boylan, "the Townsend's Gent", did little to win Edmund's confidence. In one of his letters he admitted, "I must confess that I am not desirous of having them (Brothers) permanently settled in that parish, as I think it is not the spot to begin in – May the will of God be done in it."[21] Townsend Street is near Hanover Street. Edmund's hopes seemed shaken, for on his return to Waterford from Dublin, he confided to Sister Mary Biggar, "for the last days I was a good deal occupied and, what was worse, that my spirits were for the most part as low as ditch water".[22] An undated advertisement, seeking donations, and bearing the signatures of Archbishop Murray and Thomas Sherlock, of York Street, was issued soon after the opening of Hanover Street.[23] I quote one sentence:

In order to render this admirable Institution permanent among us, and to diffuse, as widely as possible, among the

Poor, the benefits which it is calculated to impart, it was deemed an object of the highest moment, to procure more capacious School Rooms, and also a commodious residence for the Teachers, where they would be joined by new Associates.

We have seen how Edmund Rice, by abdicating authority over the Brothers, and promising money to support them, ensured the school became permanent. While his name does not appear in the advertisement, its sentiments reflect his vision. We notice that one of the purposes of the foundation was to attract 'new Associates'. This ambition to attract vocations and provide for their training would figure high on both the Founder's and the Archbishop's agenda for Dublin.

Brother Grosvenor proved an able administrator and zealous teacher. The school gained a reputation for excellence, attracting numerous pupils. The conditions in which the poor lived were deplorable. "Their sufferings from want of fuel, want of water and of clothing can only be credited by those who witnessed them. The sufferings of the poor children cannot be described; many perish and those who survive are in many instances so debilitated by want as to become sickly and infirm at an early period of life."[24] Is it any wonder Edmund was determined that schools would be successful in Dublin? His heart bled with disappointment when he considered how little he could really do to relieve their hunger. Trusting in prayer he attempted the impossible.

Most of the boys lived in overcrowded, insanitary houses. School for them was an unknown experience. While the initial adaptation process may have been trying, the 'delightful' conditions of their new school certainly raised their spirits. We read in the *History of the Institute*:

> The boys were not easily managed at first, but this difficulty soon passed away, and they became docile and studious, and the improvement in a few years was so great as to attract the attention of all. The school rooms were airy and commodious and commanded a view of the canal, river and sea. The residence was pleasantly situated, and in summer was delightful; but the distance of the chapel made the walk for the Brothers in winter rather disagreeable.[25]

Edmund was happy. Mount Sion, a purpose-built school, in its own grounds, on the outskirts of Waterford, was also a delightful place. Bright, airy classrooms, in a garden setting overlooking the city, was heaven on earth to boys accustomed to squalor in poor, congested homes.

It is not our intention to provide a full chronological history of the Dublin foundations. Hanover Street, through past pupils and admirers, supplied Brothers to man these other schools. Besides Hanover Street East, schools were established in Mill Street (1818), 67 James's Street (1820), Meath Street, 42 Jervis Street (1827) and North Richmond Street (1831). All these attracted large enrolments. Like Edmund in Waterford, the Brothers provided education, clothing and food for the very poor, and others not so poor. Support for Brothers and schools came in large measure from personal resources (not very profitable), collections, annual sermons and donations from benefactors. The Hanover Street rent was paid by the Archbishop and Mr. Bacon.[26]

Grosvenor's letter, in 1814 to Father Dunn, Preston[27], gives some insight into the ideals that motivated him, ideals he learned during the ten years he lived with Edmund in Waterford:

> the Brothers educate the poor for no other motive than "pure and disinterested charity", and in so doing, "render greater glory to God"; to better fulfil this charge, "they consecrate themselves, without reserve, by vow"; they "watch over them (pupils) with truly paternal solicitude"; "this society (was) founded on charity and guided by its dictates.

As we have seen, Edmund Rice, by his generosity, ensured that the Dublin schools would be made "permanent".[28] Both he and Grosvenor frequently consulted Archbishop Murray on plans to improve the schools. Grosvenor had the welfare of the students so much at heart that he proposed shortening the four week summer vacation. The boys were brought to school for an hour on each day during their holidays, for instruction and are "examined in their tasks".[29] We might wonder what the pupils thought of this scheme. Edmund would have been less demanding. Years later, despite pressure from all authorities, he insisted that the Brothers in Gibraltar take some weeks vacation.[30] To cope with

The monastery and school at North Richmond Street, Dublin.
■ *marks the room occupied by Brother Edmund Rice 1831-1838.*

the demands of school work all teachers need some period of extended relaxation. We cannot but admire Grosvenor's zeal and commitment. Edmund's zeal was tempered with greater prudence. He realised that little progress was possible with exhausted teachers. Grosvenor actually went to an early grave, worn out by his zealous work for souls. Like Edmund, Grosvenor dutifully submitted to Church authority. In making recommendations he left the final decision to the Archbishop, "of this you are the best judge".[31]

Recommendations are also made to widen the curriculum by including "useful trades". "Pious young men who labour at trades" could be admitted to the Institute, requiring some changes in rule. Benefits would include promoting their own good, the children would learn trades "their morals at the same time preserved", prove an auxiliary to the funds, induce parents to keep their children at school. Besides suggesting some mechanism for supervising the schools, he feels very strongly that each school should have one or two priests attached, "Such was Rev. Dr. Hussey's design". The Brothers do not have it in their power to promote the moral improvement of the pupils "effectively" until this is done.

Under the directorship of Grosvenor, Hanover Street school attained an enviable reputation for excellence. Of all the schools in Dublin Archbishop Troy stated in 1816 that the school was 'pre-eminent'.[32] From an initial enrolment of 150[33] the numbers grew to several hundred within a few years.[34] In 1818 five hundred boys were on the roll, being taught by six Brothers.[35] Warburton continues: "In the school at Lime Street are six Brothers who live in seclusion and community. Some of them are very young and all of them gentlemen in independent circumstances. They voluntarily left the world, without entering Holy Orders, at a time when others begin to enjoy it, and feel more pleasure in the society of the poor children they instruct, than in any other source of social enjoyment." In that year the second Dublin school was established in Mill Street.[36]

Loss of Grosvenor
However some causes of dissatisfaction arose in Hanover Street. In his letter (4 April 1815) to the Archbishop Grosvenor states,

"I also send you the letter which contains the agreement of the Waterford community relative to our stipend. It is probable, my Lord, that they will never be content with less than my removal from Dublin. It may perhaps be the only means of establishing unanimity."[37] The need for his removal seemingly stemmed from the question of the stipend, which put a strain on resources reducing the Waterford community 'to distressing economy'. It is significant that Bishop Power wrote to Dr. Murray the following week regarding the original agreement. With four Brothers then in Hanover Street the need to maintain Grosvenor there could have been deemed unnecessary.

Grosvenor had made recommendations to Archbishop Murray regarding changes in the Rule.[38] Were the Waterford Brothers unhappy with these? Did the suggestion that priests be introduced into the society cause extreme annoyance? Whatever the reason, Grosvenor at all times displayed remarkable patience and humility.

Grosvenor continued: "Candour also obliges me to confess it would be more agreeable to my inclinations, rather to separate from the Institute, but your determination shall alone settle my choice – confiding that the mercy of God will enable me to support all the consequences. I have given you much trouble, my Lord, indeed much against my will, but Our Lord I hope will reward the patience with which you have borne with me."[39]

Grosvenor remained a faithful Brother until 1821 when he left to study for the priesthood. After ordination he taught for some time in a "renowned classical school" at 64 Jervis Street.[40] His last two years were spent most selflessly in Irishtown, spending ten hours daily in the confessional. When teaching in Hanover Street, he left little time for relaxation. As a priest he was the same. He died on 4 November 1827.[41] His memorial tablet in Donnybrook church describes him thus:

> In him society possessed a member ever active to promote its best interests; Youth found him a wise and gentle instructor; the unfortunate a friend, the poor a parent.

Roman Brief

As early as 1810 Edmund Rice wrote to Archbishop Bray, of Cashel and Emly, with an eye to a foundation in Thurles, "I trust

Archbishop Troy

Archbishop Murray

Fr. Kenny, S.J.

Hanover Street, Dublin

in the goodness of God that it (the Institute) will spread before long in most parts of the Kingdom (Ireland and England)."[42] In 1811 Grosvenor was in communication with Fr. Dunn regarding a foundation in Preston.[43] In 1812 another step in that direction was taken with the foundation in Dublin. The first school outside Ireland, in Preston, was not until 1825.[44] The delay was due to a shortage of personnel, lack of money, and a cumbersome system of inter community, and inter diocesan, transfers. In his letter[45] to Doctor Murray Grosvenor referred to "an arrangement which took place in Waterford relative to the changing of subjects, or rather sending them as missionaries – experience teaches us that some more clear and correct rule would be necessary on that subject".

When Dr. Murray returned from Rome in 1817,[46] he brought a copy of the De La Salle Brothers' rule for inspection. Diligent study and interchange of ideas took place over the next few years, the opinions of the Brothers being sent to Edmund in Waterford.[47] The letter of application, undated, and without a source address, signed simply by Edmund Rice was forwarded to Rome.[48] This application caused much soul stirring among the Brothers, positive opposition from Bishops Walsh and Murphy, of Waterford and Cork respectively. However, the support of the majority of the hierarchy, canvassed by Archbishop Troy, accompanied the application, endorsed especially by the two Dublin bishops.[49] On 5 September 1820 Pope Pius VII, approved the constitutions of the new congregation with the Bull, *Ad Pastoralis Dignitatis Fastigium.*[50] This was a magnificent achievement for Edmund Rice. Its prompt approval was made possible through the help of the Dublin Bishops. Dr. Murray's letter (CT31) to Edmund Rice clearly showed his "much pleasure" at the Pope's approval. The Archbishop's vision, like that of Edmund, is not confined just to Dublin. "God grant stability to an Institute that promises so fairly to be of essential benefit to the interests of religion in this country."

The Papal Brief was certainly Edmund's greatest achievement. It could not have been realised without support in Dublin. In fact Edmund referred to a "religious Society which flourishes in Dublin and in other parts of Ireland"; Archbishop Troy gives a slightly different twist to this phrase by referring to good "for Religion not only in Dublin but also in other parts of this Kingdom".[51]

Royal Commission

In 1825 a Royal Commission on Education visited Hanover Street.[52] The superior, Brother Michael B. Dunphy, who was examined by the Inquiry welcomed them to the school. They reported:

> We have visited one of the Dublin schools, situated in Hanover Street East... It contains, in four apartments, between four hundred and five hundred children, Mr. M. B. Dunphy having been appointed Director by Mr. Rice; there are also three other teachers who are Brothers of the Congregation. The system of education is prescribed by Mr. Rice, and he also appoints the persons assisting him, and is the same in all the schools established under the Institute.

The curriculum included catechism, elements of arithmetic, grammar, book-keeping, navigation, algebra and geometry. The commission continues:

> During the time of attendance in this, as well as in the other schools of the Fraternity we have visited, the children are kept in good order, and the Masters seldom have recourse to corporal punishment. Mr. Dunphy states in his evidence before us that, although the first object of the Congregation is the education of the children and instruction in the Roman Catholic Religion, they are not prohibited from giving literary instruction to Protestants, and that they teach charity and goodwill to mankind without distinction of religion.[53]

As elsewhere the Brothers conducted schools on Sundays, at night for apprentices and parents, besides operating a lending library, an unknown amenity in most schools in Dublin at the time.[54]

Inter alia in an appeal for Hanover Street in 1824 the academic successes of the school were listed. Past pupils secured responsible employment, "and some have been selected to conduct other schools established for the education of the poor who are found to be well calculated to fill so important a position."[55] Provision of further schools depended on sufficient Brothers. Why should young men enter a vocation that promised little more than hard work and poverty? Rev. Joseph Butler DD, OCC, a past pupil of Limerick recalls: "It is with heartfelt pleasure I recall to mind many of the Christian Brothers whom as a pupil I knew. Some of these were novices under their saintly founder who must have had a fascinating manner and impressive bearing to attract those early followers of his to the lowly and irksome duty of instructing the poor, ignorant and barefooted children who crowded into their schools."[56] Due to necessity the Brothers' fare was meagre. Kate Graham whose uncle (unidentified) was one of the pioneer Brothers informs us, "They (early Christian Brothers) led holy and abstemious lives and it is not too much to say that they got the spirit that animated them from Brother Rice."[57]

In the Presentation period, 1812 to 1822, the Dublin communities had to recruit their own postulants. Of the known fifty-four entrants to the congregation during that decade, twelve were admitted in Dublin.[58] Excepting Grosvenor and his companion, no vow-bound Brothers were released from Waterford or elsewhere. In 1814, Edmund Rice suggested that Patrick Corbett, who sought admission to the Brothers in Carrick-on-Suir, should also join the Dublin community.[59] Corbett firmly decided to remain in Carrick-on-Suir. When Michael Dunphy applied for admission, in 1816, he would have dearly loved to live in or near the same house as his brother, Edward, then resident in Waterford. However he agreed to seek admission in Dublin.[60] Despite moral support from Edmund Rice and the three communities in the diocese of Waterford, Mount Sion, Carrick-on-Suir and Dungarvan, Dublin was singularly alone, dependent on itself for personnel and financial support.

Though isolated, the Brothers were strengthened by Edmund's abiding interest, his frequent visits, his extraordinary zeal. They were constantly in his prayers. The detailed knowledge of Dublin, as indicated in his correspondence, shows how dear to Edmund's heart the capital was. The Brothers felt assured:though far away in Waterford, Edmund was their guiding light, their exemplar. They knew he was with them in spirit at all times.

North Richmond Street Dublin

Daniel O'Connell, the Irish politician, famed as 'The Liberator', fought hard against the British Government to give Irish Catholics basic human, religious and civil rights. Peel, the Chief Secretary for Ireland, opposed him at every turn. O'Connell formed the Catholic Board. Peel proclaimed it. O'Connell formed the Catholic Committee. Peel proclaimed it. O'Connell set up the Catholic Association, in March 1824. It survived until Emancipation five years later. The association collected the 'Catholic Rent', one penny per month, to finance its causes. One of these was the provision of Catholic schools. In fact, £1,500 was set aside for a proposed model school in Dublin.

Edmund Rice saw great need for schools in Dublin. In the 1820s he was finalising the Brothers' Rule. In this the Brothers were urged to, "labour to procure the salvation of the dear little ones confided to their care: thus extending the kingdom of Christ and advancing more and more the Divine honour."[61] The three schools in Dublin, Hanover, Mill and James's streets, were going well. With the congregation on a firm canonical footing, since papal approval, with an establishment open in England (Preston, 1825)[62] Edmund was determined to provide more schools. The money from the Catholic Association was available to him.

With this in mind he came to spend three weeks in Dublin in February 1826.[63] One of the principal people he had to meet was Bryan Bolger,[64] a measurer (architect) who decided in 1821 to apply the residue of his property, estimated at £8,000, to Dr. Murray for the education of the poor, "and no other purpose whatever". This promise was formalised in his will, dated 26 April 1832.[65] Mr. Bolger was commissioned to find a site, in the North city, for the proposed new school.

However, Edmund's patience was to be tested. Several important meetings had to be cancelled, ill health confined him to bed.[66] He managed to get up one day and take a walk as far as the Canal docks at Ringsend,[67] then a very pleasant district. The proposed three week stay was extended. He was still in Dublin seeking a site in late July.[68] In December Edmund was making his retreat in Dublin. He wrote to communities asking the Brothers' to continue praying for success in procuring a site, "until God is pleased to hear us."[69]

In December 1826 a committee set about raising money to build a school in the Pro-Cathedral parish.[70] With the blessing of Archbishop Murray some of this money would be devoted to Edmund's school. Even before a site was secured and in anticipation of the opening of the new school, the Brothers opened a school at 42 Jervis Street, in 1827.[71] The initial enrolment of 400 soon rose to 600. Less than half the children contributed one halfpenny per week.[72] With little money coming in, Edmund, his heart ever anxious for the welfare of the children, saw that the great need outweighed any financial considerations. Speaking of Jervis Street boys, our historian tells us, "that their ignorance was truly lamentable and their general conduct in keeping with their ignorance."[73] Edmund could not sit back and see so many children deprived of education. With episcopal support, and adequate money promised from several sources, Edmund decided to press ahead. The Model School, besides catering for hundreds of children, would also serve as novitiate and training school for Brothers.

Edmund Rice and his council moved to Hanover Street East, Dublin, in 1828.[74] Though preoccupied with administrative duties, especially regarding the proposed school, Edmund, with some Brothers, visited the male patients in Jervis Street Hospital. There they met Sisters of Charity, providing the same service for the female patients. The sisters experienced some difficulty in their school in Gardiner Street, due to lack of experience, in controlling the girls. Sister Mary Xavier Hennessy asked the Founder for assistance. He said, "I'll send you Mr. Duggan." "Oh, is it that little boy?", replied the good sister. "Little boy, indeed, I wish I had fifty such little boys", was Edmund's response.[75]

Always dear to Edmund's heart was the plight of those awaiting execution. On 5 November 1829 Michael Mellon, 35, and Thomas Magrath, 25, though innocent, were found guilty of the murder of Thomas Hanlon. Seven thousand turned up two days later for their execution. The papers tell us the men were "attended by two monks from Hanover Street who were unremitting in their attention, from the moment of their condemnation until the last minute of their earthly existence".[76] Edmund Rice was living in Hanover Street at that time. If not personally involved, he encouraged the Brothers in this delicate work of mercy.

In 1828 Bryan Bolger acquired a site, in trust, for Edmund Rice, at North Richmond Street.[77] The new school was intended not just for the local parish: Murray's and Rice's vision saw its purpose as "to train up Religious Instructors for the parts of the United Kingdom".[78]

100,000 people witnessed the laying of the foundation stone of the school by O'Connell on 9 June 1828.[79] On 11 August Archbishop Murray laid the foundation stone of the residence and novitiate.[80] Building was delayed for lack of funds.[81] Archbishop Murray subscribed £20 in November 1828, being satisfied at the building's 'advanced state'.[82] Archbishop Murray's biographer tells us: "...Whilst the Christian Brothers, having lately come to Dublin, had only one still unobtrusive school for boys in a disused timber-yard at City Quay... Dr. Murray considered the Catholic educational future of Dublin assured when in 1828 – eight years after he obtained for the Congregation of Christian Brothers the approbation of Pius VII he blessed the now historic O'Connell Schools, North Richmond Street."[83]

The crowds, the speeches, did not tell the whole story. In fact, from Edmund's point of view the opening of the school was far from auspicious. Ever confident in Providence, but equally eager to see the school completed, we read that in 1828, "the founder was in great straits for funds and he had frequently to borrow".[84] These borrowings would cause extreme problems later.

A subscription list initially earned a good response. However, when the list was closed in 1831, just £472.0.6d was collected. The building of the residence was suspended early in 1829.[85] The house annalist recorded that, "There was not one pin's worth done to our new house, at Richmond Street, this year for want of funds".[86] He added that, "the completion of the monastery and school at North Richmond Street was the great desire of the Founder".[87] How must Edmund, now that he was no longer a young man, have felt at seeing, what was undoubtedly his greatest ambition, an establishment guaranteeing a steady supply of competent teachers for the schools, a structure in place to ensure the continuance of his schools, gradually disintegrating before his eyes? He could hardly believe that the new school, with funding assured, was in jeopardy, due to reneging on promises by outwardly respectable concerns. To compound Edmund's anxieties the 1829 Emancipation Bill, granting representation in parliament rights to Catholics, threatened to transport all vow-bound religious from Ireland and England. Edmund's advice to the Brothers was: "Be intent on prayer".[88] Is it any wonder that from 1828 to 1831 he had 2,773 Masses[89] celebrated for the success of the North Richmond Street project? To compound

Edmund's problems some Brothers demanded that a Chapter be called to discuss outstanding differences in the Institute. This Chapter was less than a pleasant experience for Edmund. Though held in Waterford, coinciding with the uncertain political situation and the ongoing problems in Dublin, the untimely combination of events caused Edmund's health to deteriorate. He tendered his resignation as Superior General to the Chapter.[90] He was unanimously requested to remain in office. Fortunately, after a brief holiday, his strength was restored.[91] He attended to the needs of the poor with renewed diligence.

Some hope for a steady income arose when the Governing Body of the Cemeteries Trust signed a deed in support of North Richmond Street school in March 1830. The expected money did not materialise.[92] Even the Corporation refused to supply water to the school. A well on the site proved more than adequate to supply both residence and school.[93]

Edmund Rice sent Brother Francis Thornton to England to collect funds in 1830 and 1831.[94] £500 was collected. On 9 June 1828 Bryan Bolger made over £1,000, by bond, to Edmund Rice for the school.[95] This £1,000 proved a God-send to Edmund; he was able to complete both house and school. Some years hence, this same £1,000 caused serious legal difficulties leading to the eventual mortgage of the premises.

While Edmund was worried about North Richmond Street, the existence of the schools in the Liberties was in jeopardy. The Brothers took over schools at 67 James's Street in 1820, and lived in a house on the site. For economic reasons, they returned to live in Mill Street in 1829, but remained teaching in the school. The school was attached to the National Board in 1832. The Brothers withdrew.[96] The new Parish Priest of Francis Street, Matthew Flanagan, gave little support to the Brothers in Mill Street, even at their annual sermon.[97] A Brother in the community complained that a solid foundation for the school had not been laid, thus creating financial difficulties. Even though they were experiencing difficulties, he concludes his letter by stating: "God will always protect and deliver us from our difficulties in His own good way and time".[98]

The period of uncertainty and concern was temporarily forgotten on 23 June 1831. Brothers Rice, Dunphy, Ellis, Duggan and four novices, Hoare, Ryan, Fitzgerald, Maher, took up residence in the new dwelling house in Richmond Place.[99] On 11 July, 600 pupils were transferred from Jervis Street to the new school. The Jervis Street school was then closed.[100]

On his way from Mill Street to Mass in Francis Street Church, Edmund distributed "alms, as was his custom, to all the poor people he met on the way, and at the door of the Church". Even when at prayer he noticed the piety of the people around him. One girl edified him deeply: "Oh! Brother Stanislaus, did you notice that child this morning at Holy Communion? – I was deeply impressed by such faith and piety in one of her tender years."[101]

Fuller accounts of the early history of North Richmond Street are available elsewhere. From the beginning the school attracted more pupils than it could accommodate. Tributes to the excellence of the education provided were paid by visitors, representing Church and State. In 1832 the school was attached to the National Board.[102]

Despite all his other commitments Edmund Rice found time to take classes in Richmond Street. Some of the most tender recollections of him as a teacher belong to that period. "The people had the idea that when their children were under Brother Rice that they would be well looked after: and he was very kind and lovable to children and his good name lived after him". Mrs. Anne McDonald, who had sons in the school, speaks of Edmund: "The people loved him and thought him a saint, he did such wonders for the children of his time. Nothing would vex or disturb Brother Rice. He told me not to be vexed when he would not punish the boy (her son) for me. Brother Rice was very good natured. It was in his face."[103]

Edmund's charity was not confined to the classroom. Brother Stephen Carroll recalls: "The day I had the happiness to enter the Novitiate, a Dublin lady told me, that lived near Gardiner Street Church: "Mr. Rice is the great landmark – when he stands up, all the Monks stand up and when he kneels, all kneel; and when he retires, all do the same". And though Richmond Street was not-to-say very far from the Jesuits' church, for an old man like him it was no small distance, still he was very seldom to be seen absent though very heavy on his feet at the time. And as for the number of poor people he relieved on his way to and from Mass, but few can tell."[104]

The National Board

As early as 1814 Brother Grosvenor was in London exploring the possibility of receiving State aid. He reported, "It is probable that the legislature may see the propriety of granting the Society aid in some shape, to promote its useful labour. An exertion will be made to obtain it".[105] It is likely that Edmund supported this inquiry. It is interesting to note that they were not averse to accepting aid, even from the 'legislature'.

The 1824-25 Royal Commission into Education in Ireland was set up at the request of the Irish Catholic Bishops. The Brothers, represented by Bernard Dunphy, were given a very fair hearing. While the Commission established that Catholic schools were excellent, the need to support them financially became obvious. However, help was not immediately forthcoming. The National Board of Education was established by Chief Secretary Stanley in 1831.[106]

Archbishop Murray enthusiastically supported the new Board, being one of the Commissioners.[107] Edmund Rice connected six schools, including the two Dublin schools, North Richmond Street and Mill Street, with the Board, in June 1832. One of the Board's inspectors, John F. Murray, gives this report on the former school in 1835:

> It is quite enough for the inspector to say that he observes in this excellent institution, Richmond Street, Dublin, everything to admire and nothing to condemn. The inspector does not know whether to admire most the military precision with which the children are regulated and controlled, or the amazing proficiency manifested in all those branches of knowledge in which they are so ably and benevolently instructed.[108]

A lot of ink has been used to describe the anti-Catholic and anti-Irish attitude of the Board. The strong bias of the ever-growing number of Brothers, following the Riordan-Leonard influence, vigorously promoting a rigid interpretation of the vow of gratuitous instruction, opposed the Board. While the 1836 Chapter, held in North Richmond Street, was called to elect an assistant in place of Austin Dunphy, the opportunity was availed of to direct unanimously that the Brothers' schools would sever their connection with the Board.

The decision of the Chapter was not as rigid as is usually represented. Schools which could prove, "that adequate means for the subsistence of the community either actually exist or can be supplied the connection shall be dissolved at the termination of the present half year".[109] Following these criteria the two Dublin schools were withdrawn. We can wonder if Edmund had reservations about the conclusion of the Chapter sub-committee which decided that the two Dublin schools had 'adequate means'.

Unfortunately, possibly due to an oversight, obviously not intended as a slight, Edmund did not inform the Archbishop of the decision until six months later. His letter, dated 4 June 1837, concludes with a most sincere apology, "If this step should be disagreeable to Your Grace I shall be very sorry for it." In fact Edmund was implementing a decision of the Chapter. His delay in informing the Archbishop, coupled with his sincere sorrow, "if this step should prove disagreeable"[110] may indicate that he was prepared to give the Board a longer trial. Murray was certainly annoyed. He discontinued his annual £40 subscription to Hanover Street, which ironically was not connected with the Board.[111] This was the most serious disagreement between the Archbishop and the Brothers. Years later, Father Cooke of Waterford, writing to Father Kirby in Rome, summed up the situation well:

> They (Brothers) understood from him (Murray) that he would not press his own views on them, and not until he made this declaration were the schools closed, to the great joy of all the Body (Brothers) except a few uneasy spirits among them. No – their crime is not that they closed the pay schools, which would soon produce disorder amongst them, but the separating from the National Board. Even since they did this, has Dr. Murray shown his disinclination to befriend them.[112]

Mortgage
The success of the North Richmond Street school was dear to Edmund Rice's heart. In the normal course of events it should have been his greatest success, his crowning glory. At his retirement it should have been the major achievement of his life. Not only did he retire with serious unfinished business, North Richmond Street was to cause him pain and suffering when no longer in charge of the Congregation.

146

Fuller accounts of what became known as the mortgage case can be read elsewhere. Here just a brief summary is offered.

Bryan Bolger signed a bond on 9 June 1823, giving £1,000 at 5 per cent to Edmund Rice, Edward Dunphy and Patrick Ellis.[113] In 1832 he made his will bequeathing his estate, £8,000, to Archbishop Murray, with Edmund Rice and Michael Dunphy as legatees.[114] He died two years later.[115] Brother Myles Ignatius Kelly was appointed executor.[116] The Founder was confident that Bolger's bequest would ease the financial burden on North Richmond Street.

Bolger's relatives were disappointed with the will, having justified claims on the estate.[117] Two nephews, John and James Bolger, made their complaints known, the former to the Archbishop,[118] the latter through the courts.[119] The Court of Chancery put a stay on the execution of the Bolger Will.[120] This inconvenience could have been handled. However, all Bolger's assets, including the 1828 bond, £1,000, plus interest at 5 per cent from that date (£302.9.4), were called in.[121] This money had been spent on the building. The Brothers did not possess any other surety to meet the court's demand.

Following severance with the National Board and not opening a pay school, North Richmond Street community was in financial difficulties. The number of students was reduced from 600 to 300.[122] We can well imagine how badly Edmund felt seeing so many boys deprived of schooling, and in his opinion, unnecessarily.

That same year the Commissioners of Charitable Donations and Bequests, on learning of the Bolger situation, demanded a full account not only of all Brothers' property, but also of their way of living and schools.[123] The next year, 1839, Br. Riordan the new Superior General, refused to allow the sale of North Richmond Street.[124] At the same time the landlord was demanding rent.[125] On 13 June the Superior General, his council and novices, moved residence to Cork.[126]

Writing to Doctor Cullen, Brother Riordan complained:

> Shortly after my election, not content with having prejudiced me in the mind of the ex-Superior, who has been labouring under imbecility of mind for years past, they got him to oblige me and the two Assistants and novices to depart from the

house in Dublin, built for the residence of the Superior General, by withdrawing the funds that up to that time were applied to its support, under pretext of paying debts, and they got him, unknown to me, to make over to themselves the property of the Institute, under pretext of providing for debts.[127]

Brother Michael B. Dunphy put it differently:

When Edmund Rice could no longer fund North Richmond Street, 'Mr. Riordan and Mr. Leonard both ran away to Cork, rather than quest in Dublin for its support.'[128]

We have seen that Edmund borrowed money to support North Richmond Street. However, on retirement, he ensured that all his debts be paid. The guarantees of the Catholic Association, the cemeteries committee, the Bolger bequest, parochial collections, fell far short of expectations. Assets, like Callan rents etc, were used to repay loans. Edmund applied the same strict demands of justice, he learned from his father, to his own business affairs.[129] He instructed his executors to clear all debts.[130]

The legal, and moral, position required that moneys due to the Bolger estate be repaid; in this case the £1,000 and interest. The Commissioners, rightly, had the obligation to see that moneys intended for charity be expended on the named purpose. Bolger bequeathed his money to the Archbishop for education. Neither the Brothers nor the North Richmond Street establishment were mentioned as beneficiaries.[131] The executor, Brother Kelly, realised that the only way the courts' demands could be met, and at the same time save the school, was to mortgage the school.

Both Edmund Rice[132] and Michael Riordan[133] consulted theologians and lawyers on their conscientious obligations. Unfortunately, Brother Riordan did not furnish all the facts to these experts. He was convinced that a mortgage was unnecessary. Edmund Rice, after presenting fuller information, received different advice. He realised that a mortgage was the only solution. On 11 June 1840 Brother Riordan formally forbade the executors to carry out the mortgage.[134] A religious who disobeys a formal request of a superior is guilty of serious sin. In Edmund's eyes the demands of justice, fulfilling the commandments of God, took precedence over the commands of a religious superior.[135]

On 7 July 1840 Edmund Rice and Edward Dunphy signed the mortgage, to Myles Kelly.[136] The other legatee, Patrick Ellis, did not sign. North Richmond Street school was saved.

Following the signing of the mortgage, further opinions, both theological and legal, were sought. In a letter to Archbishop Murray Edmund wrote: "I trust I Have done no more in this affair than justice called upon me to do... I will submit to your Grace if (I am) liable to the imputation of disobedience under the circumstances detailed in the statement to which the opinion of Father Colgan is the answer".[137]

Colgan[138] was of the opinion that Rice had no option but to sign the mortgage.

Father Kenney sj[139], briefed by Brother Riordan, did not feel that the mortgage was necessary. In a letter to Dr. Murray he referred to the Founder:

> I would give all the money at stake in this business to have prevented one of the obligers from signing the Mortgage. I feel too strongly the influence of that act on the high reputation of him to whom you are all so much indebted.[140]

It was sad that one of Edmund's greatest friends and admirers, through misinformation, was forced to hold him in so low esteem.

A lot more could be written about this affair. I will conclude with the decision of the 1841 Chapter, held in Mount Sion. The four protagonists in the affair were Edmund Rice, Michael Paul Riordan, Edward Dunphy and Myles Kelly. The last three being present, gave their version of events to the Chapter. The Founder was refused admission. The Chapter decided that, "...Austin Dunphy, having signed the deed of mortgage under the advice of a theologian and that the said signature was an act of justice, was not guilty of disobedience. The Brothers, having also considered some matters of difference between Brother Ignatius Kelly and the Superior (Riordan), believe both acted conscientiously and recommend to bury the whole matter in oblivion."[141]

Riordan, Dunphy and Kelly were exonerated by name. Edmund Rice was not mentioned. However his name was also cleared, if only through implication.

Pay School Controversy

Edmund was determined that the Dublin mission should succeed. With the Archbishop's support Edmund gave the National School system a fair chance. The 1836 Chapter decided to disconnect the schools. Again Edmund had a difficulty: how to support the schools? He had a solution: pay schools. He gave less consideration to "the magnitude of the obstacles than the means of overcoming them."[142] Pay schools were always on Edmund's agenda. He seriously promoted them when all else failed.

The Presentation Rule, adopted in 1808, prescribed that poor children only be admitted to the Brothers' schools.[143] Where no provision was made for boys 'in easy circumstances' pay schools were allowed[144], the profits being devoted to the upkeep of the poor school. According to the Papal brief the Brothers' principal care was to teach male children, particularly the poor.[145] In the Brothers' own rule[146] they were to teach boys, "especially the poor." Note the words particularly and especially, not exclusively. Archbishop Murray was anxious that pay schools be set up. "I see schools for the poor and schools and colleges for the rich both at home and abroad; but for the middle class I see no provision made."[147]

Edmund Rice appealed to the Holy See for permission to open pay schools in January 1823.[148] Due to the opposition of Bishop Patrick Kelly, Bishop of Waterford & Lismore, the request was refused.[149] A similar fate awaited requests of 6 April 1824[150] and 22 May 1824.[151] Dr. Kelly was 'completely adverse to the application'.[152]

In January 1838 Edmund issued a circular letter[153] seeking the Brothers' advice on pay schools, as the 1836 Chapter decided to break the Brothers' connection with the National Board. The 1838 Chapter elected Michael Paul Riordan as second Superior General and allowed two pay schools in Dublin, while disapproving of them in principle.[154] Pay schools were permitted in conjunction with free schools. While providing education in their own right, their main purpose was to support the free school by their profits.[155]

Pay schools were opened in Hanover Street East and Mill Street. By September 1838, 80 students were attending the former; 43 the latter. The relatively high enrolment just a month after the Chapter's approval indicates the need that existed for such schools; we may surmise that the necessary arrangements were set in train prior to the Chapter, confident of a positive response. Fees charged were £1 per quarter, payable in advance.[156]

What turn would events have taken if Edmund was still Superior General? In retirement he had no function in the situation. In fact he was scrupulously obedient to directions of his successor and other superiors,[157] with the obvious exception of the mortgage question. However, events caused him distress. He was hurt at hearing of the divisions that arose in Dublin and elsewhere. Friendships were sacrificed, knowingly or otherwise, due to misinterpretation. We can well understand Michael Paul Riordan's annoyance when Rome sent a rescript favouring pay schools to the Archbishop[158] and not to himself. A petition for pay schools[159] and one for his removal from office[160] signed by eight Brothers in Dublin, headed by that of Edmund Rice, did little to calm tempers. Regarding the latter petition, Father Peter Kenney remarked, "I know not if I ever felt for any thing not done to myself, as I do feel to see the name of Brother Rice to that unworthy document... I found that my conscientious conviction forced me to disapprove of the conduct of the very men who were my own greatly revered friends and old acquaintances. I have been in close habits of sacred friendship with good Mr. Rice for nine and thirty years and the part he has taken with the memorialists is the only fault I had ever to complain of."[161] He did not know that Edmund's signature was a forgery. He made a similar remark following the mortgage of North Richmond Street. Kenney's criticism of this 'only fault' is indeed a tremendous tribute. We do not know if Rice and Kenney ever met or corresponded again.[162]

The 1841 chapter directed that both pay schools be closed.[163] The Mill Street pay school was handed over to a Father Dowling.[164] Brother Burke registered that the pay school failed "to the great joy of Fr. Flanagan and Br. Patrick (O'Flaherty)".[165]

Back in Hanover Street Br. Bernard Dunphy's anxiety is evident in another of his letters to the Archbishop: He is anxious "to prevent as far as I can, the extinction of the Christian Schools in Your Grace's diocese". He regrets the loss of schools in Meath, James's and North Richmond streets (in part), depriving education to 480, 280 and 144 boys respectively, '904 abandoned by our Brothers in want of funds'. The imminent closure of Hanover Street pay school will increase the number by 110 to 1014. Hanover Street and Mill Street schools teach 390 and 400 boys respectively.

The 'melancholy number' of abandoned boys will increase by 180 to 1194. With the closure of Ennis (400), Mill Street (400) and Hanover Street (300), the total number of boys deprived of education would reach 2,204. All these schools could be saved with a small pay school attached to each establishment. Bernard adds that financially the future looks bleak: subscriptions cannot be expected; benefactors, one offering 'some hundreds of pounds', another 'a large sum', and supporters of the pay schools, 'indignant' at their closure and Riordan's attitude, have informed him that no money will be forthcoming.[166]

With no pay school, no state grant, public confidence eroded, the Hanover Street school committee inserted an advertisement in the *Freeman's Journal*, on Thursday, 11 January 1844, announcing a charity sermon the following Sunday. The advertisement emphasised the 'gratuitous' element of the education. "An appeal is made to public benevolence on behalf of the above Institution which has afforded for upwards of thirty years a gratuitous education to thousands of poor children – an education which renders them virtuous, industrious and intelligent."

With little income, heavy rents, the withdrawal of sub-tenants, Mrs. Crotty, the proprietress repossessed the Hanover Street premises. The school was no more. Dean Meyler built commodious schools, connected with the National Board, at the rear of Westland Row Church.[167]

The closure of Hanover Street caused bitter disappointment to the Brothers, the local people and the clergy. Considering Archbishop Murray's high hopes that obtained thirty years previously, describing his attitude as disappointment would be an understatement. However, twenty years later the Brothers returned to Westland Row parish. Here Edmund Rice's sons have provided education for an unbroken period of more than 125 years. Sisters of Mercy and Christian Brothers have combined forces to run the school established by Catherine McAuley in Baggot Street. Catherine and Edmund must view this development with satisfaction from their perch in heaven.

When Edmund sent the pioneering Brothers to Dublin there was but one convent school in the city, that of the Presentation Sisters at George's Hill, founded in 1794 by Teresa Mullally (1728-1803) during the lifetime of Nano Nagle. Teresa was most diligent in teaching the children and supporting the Sisters. While her commitment to the school was absolute, she never joined the Presentation sisters nor became a vowed religious.[168]

However Edmund became intimately associated with three of Ireland's greatest foundresses, who made their first foundations in Dublin. His friendship with Archbishop Murray, and the latter's passionate support for the nuns, brought him into constant contact with them. We refer to Mary Aikenhead (1787-1858), Frances Ball (1794-1861) and Catherine McAuley (1778-1841), foundresses of the Sisters of Charity (in 1815, approved 1834), the Loreto Sisters (Institute of the Blessed Virgin Mary in 1821), and Sisters of Mercy (in 1827, approved 1841), respectively. Edmund sent a letter to Rome supporting Catherine McAuley's request for Papal recognition.[169] Each of these congregations had foundations in Westland Row parish, where Hanover Street East schools were also located.

Epilogue

In his correspondence with Edmund Rice Bishop Daniel Murray always displayed enthusiasm and tangible interest in the work of the Brothers. The magnanimous letter of Edmund Rice, dated 20 May 1813[170], in which jurisdiction over Brothers in Dublin was transferred to the Archbishop, besides a promise of continual financial support, was the guarantee they needed. Dr. Murray immediately confirmed the plan to establish the school and residence at Hanover Street East. The Institute was thus 'made permanent' in Dublin. With the advent of new members, Dr. Murray personally officiating at their professions, his plans for the promotion of elementary education were strengthened. Through his instrumentality three congregations of Sisters, Charity, Loreto and Mercy, were established in his diocese. He reposed great hopes in the Brothers. If Edmund Rice had his way more of his plans might have been realised.

The Archbishop's vision is not confined just to Dublin. "God grant stability to an Institute that promises so fairly to be of essential benefit to the interests of religion in this country."[171] On balance it might be said that Edmund's failures in Dublin outweighed his successes. Daniel Murray could reasonably feel disappointed. When the Brothers withdrew from the National

Board Edmund is quoted as saying, "Providence will be our inheritance."[172] This trust proved true, though not in the remaining years of either the Founder or the Archbishop.

Extraordinary expansion came about under Doctor Murray's successor, Cardinal Paul Cullen. In the course of ten years schools were opened in the Archdiocese in James's, Strand, Synge and Brunswick streets, St. Mary's Place, Westland Row, Kingstown, Athy, orphanages in Artane, Carriglea Park, Glasnevin, a school for the deaf in Cabra, the novitiate was established in North Richmond Street, moving later to Belvidere House, Drumcondra.

Sources

Bibliography:

A Loreto Sister *Joyful Mother of Children* Dublin, 1961.
Burke J. D. *History of the Institute* Volume 1. Dublin
Carey F. P. *Archbishop Murray of Dublin* (1768-1852) Irish Messenger Office 1951
Christian Brothers *The Educational Record* (in progress)
Donnelly N. *A Short History of Some Dublin Parishes* 1917
Fitzpatrick J. D. *Edmund Rice* Dublin, 1945
Gillespie William *The Christian Brothers in England* 1825-1880, Bristol, 1975
Kavanagh J. *The Catholic Case Stated*, Dublin, 1859
Meagher William, *Notices of the Life and Character of His Grace Most Rev. Daniel Murray*, Dublin 1853.
Normoyle M. C. *A Tree is Planted*, 1976
Normoyle M. C. *Companion to A Tree is Planted*, 1977
Normoyle M. C. *The Roman Correspondence*, 1978
Normoyle M. C. *Memories of Edmund Rice*, 1979
O'Toole A. L. *A Spiritual Profile of Edmund Ignatius Rice* Volume 1, Bristol, 1984
O'Toole A. L. *A Spiritual Profile of Edmund Ignatius Rice* Volume 2, Bristol, 1985
Rules and Constitution of the Society of Religious Brothers, Dublin, 1832
S.A. *Mary Aikenhead, Her Life, Her Work, and Her Friends*. Dublin, 1879
Warburton, Whitelaw and Walsh, *History of Dublin*, Dublin, 1818.

Abbreviations

ATIP	A Tree is Planted
CCDB	Commissioners of Charitable Donations and Bequests.
DDA	Dublin Diocesan Archives.
DLS	De La Salle Archives, Via Aurelia, Rome.
EdR	Educational Record.
GA	Generalate Archives (Christian Brothers)
LDSC	Lettere e Decreti della Sacra Congregazione (Propaganda Fide, Rome).
PRO	Public Records Office.
SCRI	Scritture Riferite nei Congressi, Irlanda (Propaganda Fide, Rome)

SORGC   Scritture Originali Riferite nelle Congregazioni Generali (Propaganda Fide, Rome).

References

1 *Reportorium Novum*, Vol. 2, No 2 p. 382.
2 Extracts from the Gilbert MSS Vols. 68, 69, Pearse Street Library, Dublin.
3 *A Tree is Planted*, page 98.
4 *History of the Institute*, Volume 1, page 423.
5 E. Rice to Archbishop Thomas Bray, 9 May 1810, Cashel Diocesan Archives.
6 Rules 2,2.
7 Edmund Rice to Pope Leo XII, 6 April 1824 SCRI, Vol. 24, F.321.
8 Edmund Rice to Pope Leo XII, 22 May 1824 SCRI, Vol. 24, F.101.
9 E. Rice and Assistants to Pope Leo XII, 20 December 1824 SCRI, Vol. 24, F. 321.
10 *Memories of Edmund Rice* page 245
11 E Rice to Archbishop Thomas Bray, 9 May 1810, Cashel Diocesan Archives.
12 Ibid.
13 *History of the Institute*, Volume 1, page 23.
14 Edmund Rice to Archbishop Murray, 20 May 1813, DDA.
15 Ibid.
16 *History of the Institute*, Volume 1, Page 23.
17 Normoyle M. C. *The Roman Correspondence*, 1978, page 378ff.
18 Meagher, op. cit.
19 Edmund Rice to Archbishop Murray, 20 May 1813, DDA.
20 Bishop Power to Archbishop Murray, 8 June 1815, DDA.
21 Edmund Rice to Mother Mary Biggar, 20 December 1813, GA.
22 Ibid.
23 Normoyle M. C. *The Roman Correspondence*, 1778, page 378.
24 Life and Work of Mary Aikenhead. quoted in ATIP, page 99.
25 *History of the Institute*, Volume 1, page 24.
26 ATIP, page 99.
27 Gillespie, page 15ff.
28 Normoyle M. C. *The Roman Correspondence*, 1978, page 378ff.
29 J. B. Grosvenor to Archbishop Murray, 27 March 1815, DDA.
30 E. Rice to Brother Patrick O'Flaherty, 28 .June 1837, Original EdR 1897.
31 J. B. Grosvenor to Archbishop Murray, 27 March 1815, DDA.
32 Relatio of Dr. Troy to Rome, 20 August 1816. SORGC 1818, Vol. 919, F. 43-4.
33 *History of the Institute*, Volume 1, page 24.
34 *Relatio* of Dr. Troy to Rome, 20 August 1816. SORGC 1818, Vol. 919, F. 43-4.
35 Warburton, Whitelaw and Walsh, op. cit. Vol 11, p. 811-12.
36 *History of the Institute*, Volume 1, page 40.
37 J. B. Grosvenor to Archbishop Murray, 4 April 1815, DDA.
38 Ibid.
39 Ibid.
40 *Dublin Morning Register*, 4 December 1826.
41 Ibid., 7 November 1827.
42 E. Rice to Archbishop Thomas Bray, 9 May 1810, Cashel Diocesan Archives.
43 Fr. Dunn to Archbishop Curtis, Armagh, 17 June 1825, GA.
44 *History of the Institute*, Volume 1, Page 98.
45 J. B. Grosvenor to Archbishop Murray, 27 March 1815, DDA.
46 *History of the Institute*, Volume 1, page 34.
47 Text in *Companion to A Tree is Planted*, page 35-6.

48 E. Rice's application to Rome for a Brief. SORGC, 1821,Vol 926, Pt. 2, Fol. 146-8.
49 Ibid.
50 LDSC, 1820, Vol. 301, F.620, 26 August 1920.
51 E. Rice's application to Rome for a Brief. SORGC, 1821, Vol 926, Pt. 2, Fol. 146-8.
52 *History of the Institute*, Volume 1, page 83ff.
53 *History of the Institute*, Volume 1, page 86-7.
54 *History of the Institute*, Volume 1, page 94-5.
55 *The Dublin Patriot*, 24 January 1824.
56 *Memories of Edmund Rice* .page 28
57 *Memories of Edmund Rice* page 120-121.
58 EdR 1979, *The Early Brothers of the Society of the Presentation*, W. A. O'Hanlon
59 E. Rice to Br. Hogan, Carrick-on-Suir, 24 May 1814. Text in EdR 1894, page 435.
60 EdR 1979, *The Early Brothers of the Society of the Presentation*, W. A. O'Hanlon
61 Rules 11,13.
62 *History of the Institute*, Volume 1, page 98.
63 E. Rice to Bryan Bolger, 5 March (1826) GA.
64 E. Rice to Bryan Bolger, (undated) (1826) GA.
65 Bryan Bolger to E. Rice, 5 March (1821) GA.
66 E. Rice to Bryan Bolger, 5 March (1821) GA.
67 E. Rice to Bryan Bolger, 8 March (1826) GA.
68 E. A. Dunphy to De La Salle Superior General, 28 July 1826. DLS.
69 E. Rice to Br. Patrick Corbett, Carrick-on-Suir, 16 December 1826. GA.
70 *Dublin Morning Register*, 4 December 1826.
71 *History of the Institute*, Volume 1, page 110.
72 Jervis Street school account-book.
73 EdR 1895 pages 96-7.
74 *History of the Institute*, Volume 1, page 113.
75 S.A. *op. cit.* page 201.
76 F. A. D'Arcy in *Dublin Historical Society*, September 1971.
Also,. John Ledwidge CFC, in *Edmund #6*, February 1988.
Also,. *Dublin Evening Post*, and *The Freeman's Journal*, 10 November 1829.
77 North Richmond Street House Book of the Foundation.
78 Ibid.
79 *History of the Institute*, Volume 1, page 121
80 Ibid. page 124
81 Br. Patrick Ellis to Br. Patrick Corbett, 1 July 1828. GA.
82 North Richmond Street House Book of the Foundation.
83 Carey, op. cit. page 161.
84 EdR 1895 page 106.
85 E.A. Dunphy to De La Salle Superior General, 16 October 1829.
86 EdR 1895 page 81.
87 EdR 1895 page 106.
88 Fitzpatrick, op. cit., page 207.
89 ATIP page 214-215.
90 E. Rice's resignation as Superior General 1829. GA.
91 *History of the Institute*, Volume 1, page 147
92 CCDB Archives, 20 November 1838. Listed under 'Charities'. Also, Burial Ground Committee to E. Rice, 27 October 1834, GA.
93 E. Rice to Water Pipe Committee, 25 May 1831. Original in EdR 1895, page 108.
94 Appeal (undated) for funds for North Richmond Street school (1828-1829) Copy in SRCI, Vol. 25, F.748.
95 ATIP page 218.

96 Donnelly, op. cit and James's Street CB annals.
97 *History of the Institute*, Volume 1, page 147.
98 Ibid. Page 149.
99 Ibld. Page 153.
100 *History of the Institute*, Volume 1, page 153.
101 *Memories of Edmund Rice* page 151.
102 *History of the Institute*, Volume 1, page 113.
103 *Memories of Edmund Rice* pages 72 and 180.
104 *Memories of Edmund Rice* pages 38-39.
105 Br. Grosvenor to Fr. Dunn, 24 June 1824 Quoted in J. Wright, Notes on the *History of St Wilfred's School, Fox Street, Preston, 1814-1914*.
106 *History of the Institute*, Volume 1, page 190.
107 *History of the Institute*, Volume 1, page 193.
108 Kavanagh, op. cit. page 420.
109 *History of the Institute*, Volume l, page 245.
110 Br. J. Leonard to De La Salle Superior General, 9 June 1829. DLS.
111 ATIP page 283.
112 Fr. Cooke to Dr. Kirby, 11 April 1842. Copy. in Archives of Irish College, Rome; Kirby Correspondence.
113 Brian Bolger Bond; Edmund Rice account book.
114 Dublin Gazett, 25 August 1835.
115 ATIP page 344.
116 *Dublin Gazett*, 25 August 1835.
117 E. Rice to P. J. Murphy, 22 January 1838 GA.
118 John Bolger to E. Rice, 19 December 1834 GA.
119 PRO Chancery Bill Book Hilary 1835-36.
120 Ibid.
121 Extract from Deed of Mortgage 7 July 1840. PRO Dublin 1840-17-256.
122 North Richmond Street House Annals.
123 *History of the Institute*, Volume 1, page 315.
124 Propaganda to Dr. D. O'Brien, Waterford 13 August 1839. APF, LDSC, 1839. Vol. 322. F.841-2.
125 M. P. Riordan to Propaganda 11 July 1839. APF, SRCI 1839-42. Vol. 27, F.112-3.
126 North Richmond Street House Annals.
127 M. P. Riordan to Dr. Cullen, 17 August 1842; Archives of Irish College, Rome.
128 M. B. Dunphy to Dr. Murray, 5 February 1842 DDA.
129 Betham extract of Wills. No.375, 21 September 1787.
130 Text of will, 26 February 1838, ATIP pages 309-310 Text. of codicils, 8 July 1840, CCDB, ATIP page 338.
131 *Dublin Gazett*, 25 August 1835.
132 Opinion of Fr. R. J. Colgan, OCC, 5 September 1840: Fr. J. S. McNamara, 7 September 1840. GA.
133 M. P. Riordan to Peter Kenney sj (undated) GA.
134 Extract from Deed of Mortgage 7 July 1840. PRO Dublin 1840-17-256.
135 Opinion of Fr. R. J. Colgan, OCC, 5 September 1840: Fr. J. S. McNamara, 7 September 1840. GA.
136 Extract from Deed of Mortgage 7 July 1840. PRO Dublin 1840-17-256.
137 E. Rice to Dr. Murray, 14 September 1840 DDA.
138 Opinion of Fr. R. J. Colgan, OCC, 5 September 1840: Fr. J. S. McNamara, 7 September 1840. GA.
139 M. P. Riordan to Peter Kenney sj (undated) GA.
140 Opinion of Peter Kenney sj, Undated, GA.
141 1841 Chapter minutes, GA.

142 Stephen Curtis, *History of the Institute*, Volume 1, page 423.

143 Presentation Brothers Rule, Part 1, chapter 1, paragraph 5.

144 Presentation Brothers Rule, Part 1, chapter 1, paragraph 6.

145 *Ad Pastoralis Dignitatis Fastigium* Brief, of Pius VII.

146 Religious Brothers' Rule (1832) Chapter 1, paragraph 1.

147 *History of the Institute*, Volume 1, page 303.

148 Holy See to Bishop Kelly of Waterford. 28 June LDSC, 1821, Vol. 304, F. 141-2.

149 Bishop Kelly to Propaganda, Rome, 13 September SRCI, 1823-27, Vol. 24, F. 137-8.

150 Edmund Rice to Holy See, 6 April 1824. GA.

151 Edmund Rice to Pope Leo Xll, 22 May 1824 SRCI, 1823-27, Vol. 24, F. 101.

152 Bishop Kelly to Holy See. 5 July 1824. SRCI, 1823-27, Vol. 24, F. 256.

153 Edmund Rice's Circular Letter, 22 January 1838. GA.

154 1838 Chapter, Minutes. GA.

155 Ibid.

156 Catholic Directory, 1841, page 444.

157 *Memories of Edmund Rice*: Brs. P. S. Carroll, page 44; T. R. Hughes, page 146; J. J. Norris, page 214; M. X. Weston, page 324.

158 Rescript favouring Pay Schools, 25 February 1841. LDSC, 1841, Vol. 325, F.149-150.

159 Memorial addressed to Cardinal Franzoni, (July 1840) DDA.

160 Petition. to Rome against M. P. Riordan. (30 July 1840) SRCI, 1839-42, Yol. 27, F. 267-8.

161 Peter Kenney sj to Archbishop Murray, 31 December 1840 and 21 January 1841, DDA.

162 Opinion of Peter Kenney sj, Undated, GA.

163 Minutes 1841 Chapter. GA.

164 Br. Ryan to Br. O'Flaherty, 7 September 1841, DDA.

165 *History of the Institute*, Volume 1, page 338.

166 M. B. Dunphy to Dr. Murray, 5 February 1842, DDA.

167 Donnelly. op. cit.

168 *Banfhondúirí Atha Cliath*, Maire B. de Paor, Dublin 1988.

169 E. Rice to Holy See (undated). SORCG, 1835, Vol. 950, F. 186.

170 Edmund Rice to Archbishop Murray, 20 May 1813, DDA

171 Archbishop Murray to Edmund Rice, 3 October 1820. EdR 1894, page 438.

172 *History of the Institute*, Volume 1, page 271.

A Memory that Lived and a Charity that Died

Edmund Rice and the Mendicity Institute

Seán E. Ó Cearbhaill, CFC

IN A QUIET PART of Waterford City between St. John's Bridge and what was the old Tramore Railway Station a plaque on a house reads: "Site of Mendicity Institute where Edmund Rice ministered to Poor Families". This little plaque recalls a great Waterford historical initiative that blossomed on this spot and continued for some years. It also connects Edmund Rice with another of the many Charities that graced the City of Waterford in the early part of the nineteenth century. Later, he was active in administering, with others, the Mary Power Charity, the James Dunphy Poorhouse, the William Aylward Charity, the Captain Foran Charity and the Trinitarian Orphan Society (Lahert 50-52). In this paper I would like to treat of the Mendicity Institute itself and of the part played by the Founder of the Christian Brothers and of the Presentation Brothers in its life and continuity.

Waterford at the time was noted for its charity to the poor. There were probably more charitable institutions in Waterford than in any other city in Ireland. The greater part of these were privately endowed hostels providing for the maintenance and lodging of the destitute, the ill, the poor and the vagrant (Lahert 43). Many of them were founded by Waterford families in exile from the Penal Laws. Altogether there were no less than thirty one of these charitable institutions (Fitzpatrick 110). A report from the Poor Law Commissioners at a later date refers to the citizens of Waterford as being "pre-eminent in Ireland for their disposition to relieve the necessitous wants of the poor" (*Third Report*, Poor Law Commissioners, Ireland, 1836, Vol. XXX, p.104). In the early years of the nineteenth century economic depression was so universal all over the country that hordes of beggars were to be found in all the cities. It was not until the year 1821, with the foundation of the Mendicity Institute, that an organized effort was made in Waterford to eliminate street begging which had become "an intolerable nuisance" in the city (Fitzpatrick 110).

From the 1760s on, the poor in Ireland had sought to exert some influence through secret societies backed by violence or threats of violence. "As more and more people faced the possibility of actual starvation the violence increased" (Corish 154). "Ireland in the first thirty years of the nineteenth century was a violent country indeed" says Corish. It was a society poised on the brink of disaster. Part of the problem was a big expansion in population from perhaps 3.6 million in 1762 to 4.7 million in 1791 and to 6.8 million in 1821 (Connolly 26). There was a sense of insecurity that had come from the Penal Laws of the previous century. Prisons were full and people were still being transported to the penal colonies of Australia for slight offences. There were so many coercion acts and so many suspensions of the Habeas Corpus Act that there was normal government for only four to five years between 1796 and 1823 (Curtis 355). At this time outbreaks of small-pox and famine fever were frequent. There were serious fever epidemics in Waterford in 1818 and in 1822 (Power 131). There were fourteen partial or complete famines between 1816 and 1842 (Foster 320). After the fall of Napoleon there was a great fall in agriculture and the rural poor were now unemployed and flocked to the towns and cities (Connolly 21). It is amazing how Edmund Rice and the early Brothers commenced and, even more so, how they continued their work during those terrible times.

It was in this atmosphere that the Association for the Suppression of Mendicity in the City of Waterford was founded in the year 1821. It was specifically stated that its function was to "cope with the plague of beggars" (Fitzpatrick 111). The *Waterford Mirror*, 12 May 1821, describes the first meeting: "For the attainment of the above inestimable blessings to society, the Association for the Suppression and Prevention of Mendicity has been lately established in the City of Waterford. Voluntary subscriptions have been entered into, and donations presented, which do credit to the charitable feelings of the inhabitants, a commodius concern is now prepared, where sustenance, employment and the means of providing lodging, shall be afforded to all mendicants who present themselves..."

Great hope was then expressed by the newspaper that the opening of the Mendicity Institute would put an end to beggars and begging in the streets: "Let not alms then, be wasted on idleness and imposture... Let everyone make a fair calculation how much the real misery or importunity of the mendicant would force from him in the streets, and conscientiously contribute that sum to the support of the Mendicant Asylum."

The Patron of the Mendicity Institute was the Protestant Bishop; its President, the Protestant Mayor. Eight Vice-Presidents, all Protestant with the exception of the President of St. John's Seminary, together with a Management Committee, made up the first Executive Council. Edmund Rice was one of the few Catholic members on this committee (Fitzpatrick *Article* 111). An account in one of the Halliday Pamphlets describes how the Establishment was maintained. There was a membership fee of two guineas as well as donations and collections. (For an equivalent in today's money all sums should be multiplied by fifty.) There were also fines and levies from the markets imposed by the Mayor and City officials. Initially the annual income was £1000 (Halliday 1822, Vol. 1250, No.10). It was a great tribute to the charity of the people of Waterford that the Mendicity Institute, the Fever Hospital, the Trinitarian Orphan Society in Hennessy's Road were all funded mainly by voluntary local subscription at a time when there were other calls on the charity of the people to relieve poverty and disaster at home and abroad, for example, famine in the West of Ireland in 1822 and the great fire that destroyed the City of St. John's, Newfoundland in 1816 (Cowman 433).

As a social experiment, the opening of the Mendicity Institute was a tremendous success especially in its first year. Not only had this scheme the great advantage of keeping the beggars off the streets but it also provided employment which was remunerative to the Institute (or Asylum as it was called) and also to the individual worker who received a bonus for good conduct and efficiency. The women inmates were employed preparing woollen and linen fabrics for the city manufacturers. Canvas sacks and mops found a ready local market and the unskilled labour of the men contributed a steady income of about £100 to the establishment (Fitzpatrick *Article* 115). Ryland, in his *History of Waterford* (1824) pays tribute to the work: "A Mendicity Society was established in the year 1820 (1821). Previous to this period, the streets were infested with beggars, the greater part of whom were strangers to the city. This nuisance has been abated in a great measure by the exertions of the Association who expended the first year upwards of £1,000; and within the short period of three years, afforded relief to 1,300 individuals" (Ryland 203).

The Mendicity Institute was housed in a large three storeyed building between St. John's Bridge and what later became the Tramore Railway Station. All street beggars were expected to report there every morning for both work and maintenance. The house was presided over by a steward and his wife. They were employed to superintend the daily conduct of the people as well as the running of the establishment. There were two schoolrooms in the third or upper storey, one for girls and the other for boys. The boys had a paid master and assistant and the girls had a paid mistress. The middle floor was equipped with all the necessaries for combing and spinning wool, spinning and weaving wax, knitting and darning stockings at which the women were employed most of the day.

The men and boys, having swept and cleaned the city streets in the early morning before breakfast, were engaged during the day grinding oyster shells and limestone. This was considered an excellent top-dressing for the soil in farming districts. The sick were paid between 8d and one shilling and 8d a week according to the needs of each patient who had the added advantage of free professional service of doctors attending in rotation each week. Clothing was not provided for the inmates. Many people donated old clothes (*Halliday Pamphlets*, R.I.A., 1822, Vol. 250, No. 10; *First Annual Report* Mendicity Institute).

The *First Annual Report* tells also of some of the disadvantages of the establishment at St. John's Bridge. Owing to limited resources the Mendicity Institute was non-residential. This meant that the doors were closed each evening and each of the poor people had to find his/her lodging for the night. There was a lodging allowance of 2½d a week per person or 5d per family. Many sought shelter in houses in the nearby streets and lanes. Two eyewitnesses, P. J. Johnston Esq. and E. Moylan Esq., describe the housing situation in the locality: "We found the number of rooms in single houses to be six or seven. In most instances there were eight persons in each room promiscuously; in many cases they amounted to ten or twelve, all apparently objects of great destitution. We estimated the average number of persons in a single house to be from forty to fifty. In one house, in an entry off John Street, there were at the time of our visit, eighty persons residing" (*Third Report*, Poor Law Commission, Ireland, 1836, Vol. XXX).

A Memory that Lived and a Charity that Died

The Waterford Mendicity Society was powerless to redress many of these evils. They were common to every city in Ireland and England at the time. At least the Society fed, and provided some employment for these poor outcasts of society. Certainly the beggars could not complain of being hungry. There was plenty of plain but wholesome food. The First Annual Report (*Halliday Pamphlets*) gives the menu for each day. There were two meals. For breakfast there was a liberal allowance of porridge (6½ ozs of meal) and a half pint of buttermilk. For dinner each person was allowed 3 pounds of potatoes (about twelve good sized potatoes) and a pint of buttermilk or a porringer of broth. Bread and new milk were reserved for nursing children and for the sick confined to bed.

Ordinarily there was no fish or meat served. Sometimes pleasant surprises were provided by the Mayor, who, as a result of confiscations at the city markets, sent some "extra dainties for the common pot." On 2 June 1827, the Mayor sent to the Mendicity Asylum: "A carcase of lamb, a leg and two loins of mutton, a half lamb, four quarters and a leg of veal, 10d worth of bread, a pair of scales and fourteen plaice" (*Waterford Chronicle*, 9 June 1827). And on the 16 June 1827 he sent: "a whole lamb, one carcase of veal, 2/7d worth of bread and eleven eggs, all seized by the Market Jury" (*Waterford Chronicle*, 16 June 1827). Such donations, however, were not very frequent.

There were various contributions to the Mendicity from time to time. These were usually acknowledged in the local press. The confiscations at the markets were also published as a warning to offenders against the law. The following would be typical of the acknowledgements:

Mendicant Asylum: The Treasurer acknowledges the receipt of the following sums: Rev. Dean Lee (subscription 42 shillings); Joseph D. Lapham (on arbitration) 63 shillings; Lady Esmonde (subscription for 1825 and 1826) 60 shillings. (*Waterford Mail*, 20 June 1826)

Mendicant Asylum: The Steward acknowledges to have received from Thomas Walsh, baker, George's Street, 3 shillings worth of bread; from Newtown School, 16 old hats

for boys; from 12 July – 26 September 6 cwt. 2 qrs. 17 lbs.
of broken victuals; Henry Sargent, Deputy Mayor, 4 stolen
geese seized by John Kelter, bridgeman; from Edmund Rice,
50 yards of linen for the boys of the Institution. (*Waterford
Mail*, 30 September 1826).

The *First Annual Report*, from the Halliday Pamphlets (R.I.A.,
Vol. 1250, No.10) gives an account of the meeting. Evidently it was
a happy gathering of the members of the Executive and Committee
in the Town Hall on 6 May 1822. There were glowing reports.
They had a balance of £56. Five hundred and seventy five beggars
received help during the year. As of that day, 6 May 1822, there
were 265 inmates on their books. The average attendance each
day was 237, between men, women, boys, girls and children under
three years of age. There was a daily average of 17 sick people
(Normoyle, *Memories* 69). Sixteen had died during the previous
year and had been decently interred.

It was a meeting of Waterford people rejoicing at the success
of a joint and original effort to meet one of the great social
problems of the time. Its members represented all local religious
denominations. Edmund Rice was present. It was he who
seconded the first resolution of the meeting which had been
proposed by Mr. Leonard, one of the Association's most active
and Catholic supporters. The resolution was an interesting one:
"That the thanks of this meeting are justly due and are hereby
given to the clergymen of the different religious persuasions in
this city, for their zealous co-operation in forwarding the interests
of the Charity; and in particular to those gentlemen who have
undertaken the performance of divine service in the Asylum on
Sundays" (*First Annual Report* 34).

That there was a great need for the services of the Mendicity
Institute is borne out very clearly by an eye-witness account of
beggars in Waterford City, included in the *First Annual Report*:
"The city everywhere presented scenes which seriously broke in
on the comfort and harrowed up the feelings of the inhabitants and
of strangers... Many of the mendicants, themselves the victims of
disease, carried about with them the seeds of infection which was
able to lay the most vigorous constitutions in the dust... Others
among the mendicants displayed to open view the ravages of the
most loathsome distempers... The young were trained up by their

parents in the same paths of moral ruin....From quarters near and far they bent their course to Waterford where the field for Mendicity was still open to their indefatigable zeal" (quoted in Fitzpatrick 111). Altogether there were seventeen annual reports of the Mendicity Institute. Of the seventeen reports only two have survived, the first and the second. The Second Annual Report compared to the first is a sad one. It does not include either a list of subscribers nor a list of donors. Local enthusiasm had evidently lessened and local support had waned. It appears that the inmates were becoming truculent, sighing for their former 'happy days' of idleness, freedom and begging.

Failing the existence now of the subsequent annual reports, we are dependent, to a large extent on what the local newspapers might have mentioned, now and again, about the Mendicity Institute in the following years. In the late 1940's Brother J. D. Fitzpatrick tried to track down these random references in the hope of increasing our knowledge of this great and very original Waterford Charity and especially in as much as it concerned our Founder, Edmund Rice. Naturally, he was disappointed when he found that the only relevant Waterford newspapers in the National Library, Dublin or in Trinity College were the *Waterford Chronicle* for 1823 and 1827 and the *Waterford Mail* for 1823, 1825, 1826 (Fitzpatrick 118).

It is difficult to reconstruct the full story of Edmund Rice's involvement with and work for the Mendicity Institute. From the documents still extant there is evidence of his great love for the Charity and also evidence of his great generosity towards it. In the first Annual Report (*Halliday Pamphlets*) his name appears not only among the members' list of subscriptions of two guineas (100 guineas in today's money), but also on a second list he was credited with a donation of £5, one of the highest on this subsidiary list. And this was but two years after the collapse of Newport's Bank in Waterford and a marked depreciation in land values in 1821 which left Edmund Rice, in common with other land-holders of the time, with a seriously reduced income (Fitzpatrick *Edmund Rice* 238). And yet just a leaf from Edmund Rice's Account-Book for the period 1822-27, (published in Normoyle *Companion* 75-8), give a clear insight into his deep involvement with this Charity. Very many contributions from himself and from others through Edmund Rice are mentioned:

14 May 1822: Mr. Power's Charity: Mr. Power gave me for the Mendicity Society money to be given, not in his name... £50.

24 July 1822: Received from the same for the same and for other objects... £18.

From May to December 1822 Edmund Rice supplied to the Mendicity Institute: 252 yards of linen; coats for poor men; coats for little girls; cash to teachers for teaching the poor children Prayers and Catechism; timber; 53 yards of flannel; money for releasing clothes from pawn; a quarter of beef; coats and shoes; money for plastering the Mendicity; cash for the mendicants (on many occasions); money for sick children and for prayer books; 100 coal tickets; 40 pairs of breeches for mendicant boys; blankets; clothes; 119 yards of linen for poor boys; blankets and sheets; gifts of money to various poor families; etc.

Edmund Rice became Chairman of the Mendicity Society in September 1826. This, I think, highlights for us today how involved he, and his Brothers, were with the problems and needs of the local scene. The Mendicity was a dying project by this time. Edmund Rice used his influence to rally the support of his fellow citizens for the Charity. At his first meeting as Chairman the following resolution was passed: "Resolved that the grateful thanks of this meeting are justly due and are hereby given to the Society of Friends for the very liberal donation of £109-16-1½d handed to the Treasurers of this Institution by the hands of Richard Davis and Joshua Strangman, Esqrs., being the amount of a collection made at the "Friends Meeting" in this city, in aid of the exhausted funds of this Charity, which timely relief has prevented, for the present, the painful necessity of closing the doors of the Asylum."

Mr. Rice, as Chairman of the Asylum Committee, proposed the resolution:

Resolved: That our Chairman and Doctor Kenny be requested to communicate the foregoing resolution to Richard Davis and Joshua Strangman, Esqrs.

Resolved: That we earnestly entreat the inhabitants of Waterford of every other religious denomination to follow the above charitable example.

Resolved: That the foregoing resolutions be inserted in each of the Waterford papers."
– from *Waterford Mail*, 6 September 1826.

Some further references in subsequent issues of the Waterford newspapers still extant in the Waterford Municipal Library, list the continuing donations of Edmund Rice to the Institute from 1823 to 1831. The *Waterford Chronicle* in several issues during the year 1823, records, among others, his donations from May to December in that year:

> *29 July:* Two guineas and a basket of cabbage.
> *12 August:* A basket of cabbage.
> *7 October:* A quantity of onions.
> *Christmas 1823:* A quantity of pork weighing 3 quarters, 17 pounds.

That was for the year 1823. There are no copies of the Waterford newspapers for the year 1824. Several issues of the *Waterford Mail* for the year 1825 are still extant and there are a number of references to further donations from Edmund Rice to the Mendicity Institute:

> *7 September:* Two guineas and a basket of onions.
> *12 September:* A basket of onions.
> There are donations of 'a basket of onions' also for the following dates: 1 October; 3 October; 10 October; 13 October. (It is likely that there was an outbreak of scurvy at the Institute).
> – *Waterford Mail*, 19 October 1825.

The *Waterford Mail*, 16 November 1825, mentions that Edmund Rice donated a quantity of pot herbs on the 5th November and also on the 13 November. It also reports a donation of £3-8-8d from Mr. Rice to purchase clothing for the inmates. In a December issue of the same newspaper there is an acknowledgement of the receipt of a consignment of pot herbs on the 3rd, 21st and 28th December and a quantity of bread and meat.

There are many references to donations from Edmund Rice in the columns of the *Waterford Mail* during the year 1826:

> *27 January:* A quantity of bread and pot herbs.

27 March: one coat, one flannel vest, one shirt.
5 August: Mr. Rice, annual subscription of 2 guineas.
Mr. Rice's donation of £2.
per Mr. Rice from Miss Landers £1.
per Mr. Rice from John Power £1.
per Mr. Rice from Charles Bianconi £1.
30 September: 50 yards of linen for the boys of the Institute.

And the *Waterford Mail*, 27 December 1826, records that Mr. Rice sent "a live pig, weight 3 quarters, 21 pounds", (evidently for the Christmas festivities).

Again there is a gap in the heroic story of one man's efforts to save the Mendicity Institute. For the year 1827 there are almost no records of donations in the few issues of the *Waterford Chronicle* that are extant. None of the issues of this somewhat liberal paper for 1828, 1829 or 1830 have survived.

A donation of 3 guineas from Edmund Rice to the Mendicity Institute for 1830 is mentioned in an article in the *Waterford News*, in April 1949. For the year 1831 the *Waterford Mail*, 12 Feb 1831, mentions that Edmund Rice "sent 15 shirts, 65 chemises for women and 50 for girls." And later that same year the *Waterford Mail*, 20 July 1831, also states that "Mr. Rice sent his usual subscription, a donation for £2-10-0d and a load of coals."

Edmund Rice was living in Dublin at this time. He had moved to Dublin in 1828.

It is interesting to note that, at this period, £2-10-0d (2d a day) was the average annual wage for a labouring man. The salary of a teacher in the Kildare Place Society Schools was £16 and the yearly stipend of a Catholic curate seldom exceeded £20 (Fitzpatrick *Article* 120).

J. D. Fitzpatrick gives a very interesting account of the annual general meeting of the Association for the Prevention of Mendicity held in the Town Hall, Waterford, on the 30th May, 1831, where a very beautiful tribute was paid to "the Gentlemen of Mr. Rice's establishment." A resolution of appreciation was proposed and seconded by two Protestant clergymen. The proposer was the Rev. J. Lawson and the seconder was none other than the renowned historian, the Rev. R. Ryland, the author of *The History, Topography and Antiquities of the County and City of*

Waterford (1824). The resolution was as follows: "That to the Gentlemen of Mr. Rice's establishment we return our most cordial thanks, for their prompt attendance on all Sundays and holidays at the Mendicant Asylum, to impart Religious Instruction to the male part of the inmates of the establishment" (Fitzpatrick *Article* 117). Although Edmund Rice was not in Mount Sion in 1831 it is obvious that his Brothers were still in contact with the Mendicity Institute. It is nice to hear them called "the Gentlemen of Mr. Rice's establishment." To the two clergymen they were the men who were continuing the work of their Founder, Edmund Rice, for the poor and powerless.

In a postscript to a letter to Sir John Newport, dated 5 July 1830, and sent from Dublin to Waterford, Edmund Rice writes:

> I enclose you £20 which you'll have the kindness to send to the Mendicity Institute, Waterford. I have reasons for wishing that my name should not be identified with it, and therefore shall thank you not to mention it. This Institution is very dear to me, and I should feel much regret if it were to go down... (quoted in Normoyle *Companion* 347).

This anonymous subscription of £20 (worth £1,000 in today's money) at a time when he and his Congregation were in debt for the building of a Training College for their own Brothers and for Catholic Teachers in Dublin, is a measure of the faith of Edmund Rice. It is also a measure of the love he had for the poor of Waterford and for all those good people of that city, of different religious persuasions, who gave of their time and money and efforts for the Mendicity Institute. Was this the first or were there other such anonymous gifts from Edmund Rice?

When Edmund Rice retired in 1838 he left Dublin and came back to Waterford. He was 76 years of age and his health was broken. He lived at Mount Sion until his death in 1844. One wonders, if he saw it, what he thought when a large notice appeared on the front page of The *Waterford Mirror* on the morning of 3 February in the year 1840:

TO THE CITIZENS OF WATERFORD

Having been waited upon by a Deputation from the Managing Committee of the Mendicity Asylum representing that, notwithstanding every exertion on their part to obtain means sufficient to carry on the Institution, they find it impracticable to do so.

I have, therefore, most earnestly to request a Public Meeting of my Fellow Citizens, to be held at the Town Hall, 4 February, at one o'clock for the purpose of considering if any means can be adopted to prevent the fearful alternative of closing its doors, and turning out to perish on the streets the unfortunate inmates, at present consisting of the following 245 miserable beings: ten old men – some blind, decrepit and epileptic; 88 women – widows, some deserted by their husbands, and many having families of five or six children; 76 boys – many destitute orphans; 52 girls ditto, ditto; some in hospital – some cripples and incurable.

Henry Alcock, Deputy Mayor,
Mayor's Office,
January 29th 1840.

Such is the story, though incomplete, of Edmund Rice and the Waterford Mendicity Institute. It highlights the appalling standards and the living conditions of the destitute in Waterford in the 1820s. It highlights also the amazing charity of Edmund Rice and the early Brothers. Though fully employed in teaching and sometimes feeding and clothing the ever-growing number of poor boys in their schools, they made time and spared money to become involved in the griefs and anxieties of the poorest of poor families. The almost extravagant anonymous gift of £20 by Edmund Rice, at a time of great financial stress, to the failing Mendicity Institute in 1830, illustrates that, for the Founder and his men, Providence was in fact and in practice their Inheritance. Finally, it shows that, in spite of an unfortunate polarization on religious grounds among the people of Ireland in the 1820s, for Edmund Rice all was fair when it came to God's poor. The motive for all his thinking was not to get a job done – even an excellent job – but to serve Christ in the lost and the powerless ones of the people around him.

The story of Edmund Rice and the Waterford Mendicity Institute leaves us with a certain feeling, as though we had unearthed an ancient historical mosaic floor with nothing left but a few patches of rich fragments. These suggest to us something of the broad composition of his charity and of the colour and depth of his compassion. They hint at a very radical and truly prophetic expression of Christian living on the part of Edmund Rice and of "the gentlemen of his establishment." They give us a taste for more and urge us to dig deeper and to search farther.

References

Waterford Chronicle.
Waterford Mirror.
Waterford News.

First Annual Report of the Association for the Suppression of Mendicity in the City of Waterford, Halliday Pamphlets, R.I.A., 1822, Vol.1250, No.10.
Third Report, Poor Law Commissioners, Ireland, Vol. XXX.

Connolly, S.J. *Priest and People in Pre-Famine Ireland: 1780-1845.* Dublin: Gill and McMillan, 1982.
Corish, Patrick. *The Irish Catholic Experience.* Dublin: Gill and McMillan, 1985.
Cowman, Des. "Trade and Society in Waterford City: 1800-1840" in *Waterford: History and Society*, W. Nolan and T. P. Power (eds.). Dublin, 1992.
Curtis, Edmund. *A History of Ireland.* London: Metheun, 1972.
Fitzpatrick, J. D. *Edmund Rice.* Dublin: M. H. Gill, 1945
"A Lost Chapter in the Life of Edmund Rice" in Christian Brothers' *Educational Record*, 1950.
Foster, R. F. *Modern Ireland: 1600-1972.* London: Penguin Books, 1988.
Lahert, R. "Some Charitable Institutions of Old Waterford" in *Decies*, XXVIII, Spring 1985.
Normoyle, M. C. *Memories of Edmund Rice.* Dublin; Christian Brothers, 1979.
A Companion to the Tree is Planted. Dublin: Christian Brothers, 1977.
Power, P. C. *History of Waterford, City and County.* Cork: Mercier Press, 1990.
Ryland, R. H. *The History, Topography and Antiquities of the County and City of Waterford.* London: John Murray, 1824.

The Provenance of the
Carrick Portrait of Edmund Rice

Liam P. Ó Caithnia, CFC

IT MAY BE SAID in a general way that there are four kinds of portrait of Edmund Rice: that represented by the Carrick portrait, so named from its long association with the Brothers' residence in Carrick-on-Suir, Co. Tipperary, the Watson portraits, of which there are half a dozen or more – all of them late and based, apparently, on the Carrick portrait[1] – and several others, particularly those in Rome, of varying merit, often associated with a named place but never, it seems, with an artist.[2] Many of them, perhaps most, are older than Watson's well-known series of portraits. There is a fourth tradition however, or what appears to be such, because some who are familiar with the wider spectrum of Edmund Rice portraiture postulate what is occasionally termed a Callan tradition of painting. This interesting phenomenon will not be touched upon in our brief comment: it awaits a writer far better versed in the history of portrait painting in Ireland in the nineteenth century and much more accomplished than I could ever hope to be in recognising the technique, style and quality of one artist as distinct from another. Such a study would be most welcome indeed and could well be in the offing!

Of all the portraits, however, the one associated with Carrick, and commonly attributed to Robert Kennedy, appears to be the doyen and has aroused more than a little interest in the past year. One hopes to see an increase in such interest in the immediate future and a more informed appreciation of the probable genuineness of these attempts to capture something not only of the likeness but of the heart and soul of the Venerable Edmund Rice. The following very brief essay is an attempt to gather together such strands of reliable information as we now have concerning the Carrick portrait. No other likeness of Edmund Rice is of concern to us here.

It was decided, at a Chapter (a general meeting of delegated Brothers), in 1831-32 that Br. Edmund Rice, then in his seventieth year, should sit for a portrait.[3] It is not clear that he did so, nor does any portrait exist that is thought to relate to those years. Since there is no evidence that this decree was ever executed, it is not surprising that the next Chapter, 1838, passed a similar one, Br. Rice being now out of office. It has been suggested that this time the wishes of the delegates may have been respected because the next Chapter, that of 1841, decreed "that the likeness of the Founder and the present Superior Gen(eral) be carefully preserved."[4] Some would argue on foot of this, that a likeness or portrait had already been executed, otherwise what was there to preserve? I am not sure that everyone would agree. A likeness could be taken to mean either a general, unspecified similarity or a specific, painted portrait. To preserve one's likeness therefore could mean either of two things: in the general sense it could entail painting a person's portrait and so preserving the likeness, whilst in the more specific sense it might be taken to mean preserving somebody's portrait which had already been painted. This latter interpretation appears to have been the one adopted by Br. Normoyle: hence he assumes that the portrait was made after the 1838 Chapter. For those who may feel that we, in questioning it are splitting hairs, it may be well to note that Br. Rice and his successor, Br. M. P. Riordan are the two men under consideration in this decree and is it not altogether unlikely that Br. Riordan had already sat for a portrait some time before he became General? Yet their names are clearly bracketed by the delegates of the 1841 Chapter: both their likenesses were to be preserved!

There is some evidence that such a likeness "was painted in Waterford by Robert Kennedy in the later months of 1841,"[5] three years before Br. Rice's death. If so, and bearing in mind that the Chapter of 1841 ended on the 18th of August in that year it seems more than likely that the two portraits, Br. Rice's and Br. Riordan's, were painted following a decree of that Chapter – not the Chapter of 1838. Moreover we have information of such a precise nature that it is of the greatest importance in validating the source which all these comments share.

The picture, we are told, was painted in Waterford in 1841 by Robert Kennedy; taken to Dublin 23 November 1844 – freight 2/8; Mr. McDowall paid £6.15.0 for making a steel engraving of the picture, 30 November 1844; Gilt frame made for Founder's picture, £2.5.0[6].

The detail and precision of this information appears to me to

Edmund Rice: the Carrick Portrait (Js. O'Neill)

The Watson portrait

The Callan portrait (G. Martin)

The McDowall engraving from a Kennedy painting

remove some doubt concerning the relationship between the Mount Sion picture (whether or not it was Kennedy's) and the steel engraving known to many of us from the *Biographical Register* of 1845 (a supplement to the *Catholic Directory*). The assurance that such a relationship existed is that of Br. John A. Grace[7] the man responsible for the engraving in the first place.

If that be so however, there are many people who, unendowed with any great artistic perception, feel nevertheless that the Kennedy portrait, of which McDowall made the steel engraving, bears very little resemblance to the Carrick likeness. And that is the problem, for the Carrick portrait has, over many years, been assumed to be the creation of Robert Kennedy.[8] I am unsure what justification there ever was – if any – for such an assumption. When it was suggested that the two faces – that of the Carrick portrait and that of the engraving – were quite different in almost every way, it was pointed out[9] that steel engraving, at that time (1845), was still at a primitive stage of development and that the two faces might, after all, be of the same man. The matter is of very real importance to a study of all the nineteenth century portraits of Edmund Rice but this is not the place to pursue it. Among the questions that need to be asked are the following: when we are assured – as we have been – that two copies were made of the Kennedy portrait, does that necessarily mean that Kennedy himself made the two copies as well as the original? And assuming that some other artist made one or both of the copies, would they in turn be referred to as Kennedy portraits or would they bear the name of the secondary artist? The question is not purely an academic one as we shall see.

Br. Harry M. Dunkak, Professor of History in Iona College, New Rochelle, returned to the US shortly before Christmas 1992 having spent some six weeks searching for answers to questions concerning the portraits of Edmund Rice which he had come to Ireland to scrutinise. He and I, having looked closely at a number of these, had given special attention to the Carrick portrait for it was commonly assumed to be the master copy of all subsequent attempts to capture the likeness of Edmund Rice.[10] Having gazed long at it we agreed that, whatever about a relationship with the engraving, it was long overdue a cleaning and restoration. With the blessing therefore of Br. McDonnell, Provincial of St. Helen's Province, and the good will of Br. Noel McGrath, Superior of the Brothers' Community in Carrick, we brought it, on the 16th of December 1992, to Mr. Roland Hulme-Beaman, a highly professional restorer in Dublin, having assured him that Kennedy was the painter. It was retrieved on the 6th of October, '93.

From a series of comments made by Mr. Hulme-Beaman throughout the period in which he held the portrait the following appeared to me to be of some significance:

(a) the painting was in very poor condition and he did not appear to be enthusiastic about the possibility of its restoration;

(b) he remarked repeatedly that the paint was impossibly thin and wondered if Kennedy had not run out of paint?;

(c) he felt that the painting was probably an original. On further acquaintance with the portrait he expressed his conviction that it was without doubt an original;

(d) he felt the head was well painted;

(e) the right hand and the area close to it showed almost no paint;

(f) the portrait had been carelessly handled, roughly used, and torn in three or four places. One tear was over a foot long and badly 'repaired', the other was star-shaped as though the canvas had been punctured. (This became distressingly clear to Br. Dunkak and myself when the canvas was mounted on an easel and a light was played on it at a slant).

(g) worst of all perhaps, someone had attempted to clean or 'restore' the canvas;

(h) early in the course of examination the restorer found the answer to the problem that had appeared to challenge him from the outset: the thinness of the paint. Somebody had 'restored' the painting by washing it with soap[11] – a most volatile substance when applied to paint. The ill-effects of it are still visible and it may well cause further deterioration in time;

(i) the ear had been re-painted but in a very professional way;

(j) the hair also had been repainted;

(k) the restorer had no compliments for us for having allowed the frame to be *painted* gold and urged us several times not to do so again because the gold turns greyish in a short time;

(l) within a few minutes of receiving the portrait and before he had removed the canvas from its frame he withdrew a faded but very precious slip of paper from between the canvas (retro) and the upper transept of the frame. The piece of paper was an inverted triangle of perhaps 5 centimetres at base and 1.5 centimetres high.[12] On it were penned quite legibly the words '*Mt. Sion*';

(m) the restorer urged that the frame should not be painted again but that it should be gilt;

(n) only on the day that we returned to repossess the frame did he notice that it had always been too small for the portrait. There is no implied criticism of our very professional restorer in this: he had never at any time intended to work on the frame and had even suggested to us, on the night we brought it to his studio, the name of a highly-esteemed frame-maker. We are already in the process of finding a thoroughly reliable company to make a new frame that will suit our portrait in every way.

(o) but the most shattering information of all was given us when the work of restoration was already well under way: the artist *was not Robert Kennedy at all* but one Js (James?) O'Neill. The restorer drew my attention to the fact that the signature was genuine because it was painted *under* the varnish. The date was – and still remains – undeciphered. It reads 18 followed by two illegible digits.[13] The National Gallery of Ireland have kindly consented to give the matter their attention within a few weeks.

The emergence of O'Neill has given rise to a variety of questions: is his a copy of Kennedy? If so would it be customary at that time to refer to it as a Kennedy portrait or as an O'Neill? And where, meanwhile, is the Kennedy original of which O'Neill is a copy – *if* O'Neill is a copy, as it appears to be.[14]

To none of these questions do we have an answer yet! I have deliberately avoided in this very brief account the muddy waters and cross-currents of charge and counter-charge touching what Kennedy did and who O'Neill was. Too many people have committed themselves to some prejudice or other concerning the Edmund Rice portraits and I feel there is much to be said for taking each portrait in turn, confining ourselves to that and examining what is said or suggested concerning it without making any further conclusive deductions. This is so even if the evidence that is adduced is felt to be solid and reliably established and can be weighed and measured dispassionately. What has been advanced in this brief essay is of just such a nature. Roland Hulme-Beaman, a respected professional, is satisfied that the signature of James O'Neill is genuine. So too is the date, even if yet undeciphered. These things do not detract in any way from the work of Kennedy – an artist about whom and about whose work we know virtually nothing. When Ms. Carmel Meehan of the Waterford Heritage Centre very willingly undertook to check every person named Robert Ken(n)edy who was born or lived in Waterford between 1800 and 1850 she found only one – born 1809 – who, on foot of his age, might have filled the role of Edmund Rice's portraitist – and that man is not known ever to have painted anything! Happily, Robert Kennedy does not belong to this brief commentary. Whoever chooses to befriend his fair name will first have to prove that he existed,[15] that he was an artist (he is not mentioned in Strickland – no more than James O'Neill is!), that he had at some time lived in Waterford and that he painted a portrait of Edmund Rice. It is worth noting that Br. W. A. O'Hanlon, a most thorough researcher, conceded only that the picture painted in Waterford in 1841 and removed to Dublin in 1844 was *possibly* Kennedy's.

It should be said that the faded slip of paper already referred to does not *necessarily* imply that James O'Neill was a Waterford artist, although he may well have been, but it almost certainly means that the portrait was painted in Mount Sion or identified with it in some way because the name *Mt. Sion* is the only thing hand-written upon it. We have not yet checked the Waterford Heritage Centre for O'Neill but there seems no doubt whatever that he was the real painter of a portrait that has for many years been attributed to Robert Kennedy, who may indeed have painted the master portrait – if indeed there was such?

A final comment on the probable identification of the 'Kennedy' group of portraits – Mount Sion, Carrick-on-Suir and Dungarvan: since Br. Rice and his successor, Br. Michael Paul Riordan, had sat for portraits in "the later months of 1841," is there not a distinct possibility that both men sat in Mount Sion for the same artist? After all, the 1841 Chapter had been held in Mount Sion and had closed on the eighteenth of August and both men were in Waterford at that time. If so, would not the portrait of M. P. Riordan now hanging in Mount Sion repay careful study? Was it signed by Kennedy for example? If not, whom by? And when? Whatever the answer, it seems safe to suggest that, taken together, these three portraits, the Carrick and Dungarvan copies and that of Br. Riordan, should throw considerable light on the probable origin and provenance of the Mount Sion portrait and of the copies thereof.

How good a likeness of Edmund Rice is the Carrick Portrait? Assuming that the expression 'Carrick Portrait' always meant what it means now – while allowing, of course for the destructive 'improvement' of later years – I think we may rest assured that it was a very real likeness indeed. When, in 1885, more than forty years after Br. Rice's death, Fr. Richard Fitzgerald who had preached the panegyric at his month's mind, was found deep in thought before the Carrick portrait in the Brothers' residence in Carrick-on-Suir, he turned to a member of the community and said, "Oh, I knew Mr. Rice very well, he was indeed a great and holy man and it was I had the great happiness of preparing him for death."[16] I find this comment startling in its simplicity because the compassionate priest did not waste time suggesting that there was indeed a likeness when everyone could see clearly whose likeness it was albeit Br. Rice had died forty years before. I confess I am far more deeply impressed by Fr. Fitzgerald's comment than by that of Br. John Norris twenty years later who, when asked whether the person portrayed was really the Founder of the Brothers, remarked, "That's him all right."[17] We may add that the same Br. John Norris is recorded as having assured another Brother not later than 1912 that the Carrick likeness "was a very good portrait of him (Edmund Rice) as he appeared in his old age."[18] No doubt the same question was submitted to him many times and not surprisingly the *form* or the emphasis of the reply changed occasionally.

It is our happy fortune to have possession of this "very good portrait" of Edmund Rice even if there are lingering doubts surrounding its origin and creation. One can but hope that before the happy date of his Beatification we will have succeeded in answering a number of questions that still baffle us. If it be true that two copies were made of the original canvas painted by Kennedy for Mount Sion, a copy each for Dungarvan and Carrick-on-Suir, and since we are virtually certain that the canvas under discussion in this brief count-down is one of them, where are the other two? Surely even the black-and-white photograph of the so-called 'Dungarvan' portrait, now in the Generalate in Rome, is enough to convince anyone that the subject is the same man as the one we see in the Carrick canvas? And that is so even if the

Dungarvan portrait has clearly been tampered with. Would it not be excellent were we to see it coming from out the Flaminian Gate and being restored to its pristine simplicity – even to replacing that familiar white page mark in the bible on the thumb-side of Br. Rice's left hand as we see it in the Carrick portrait? Then too we might know who painted it – and when! That of course would not end our search. We still have not accounted for the original Mount Sion portrait. One wonders where that may be? But at least a search could be mounted. And what of the Thurles portrait which one rarely sees in latter years and which may well merit more attention than has ever been devoted to it?

Let us rejoice therefore in possessing the Carrick portrait and look forward to the happiness of a restored 'Dungarvan' signed by its creator – or copyist? Some day, please God, even the Mount Sion original may emerge intact. Who knows? Meanwhile, for what we have: *laudemus Dominum!*

References

1 Mr. Adrian Le Harivel, Assistant Curator in the National Gallery, had no hesitation in identifying the Carrick portrait as the original of the Watson portrait that hangs in North Richmond Street. All the Watson portraits are readily identifiable.

2 So we tend to speak of the Carrick, Dungarvan, Thurles portraits – but never a Mount Sion one!

3 *A Tree is Planted*, p. 253. Br. M. C. Normoyle accepts that a portrait was made in accordance with the decree of the Chapter but gives no evidence in support of his assertion and concludes that "it is uncertain whether it has been preserved for posterity, and if so, where it remains".

4 It is not expressly stated in *A Tree* that the Chapter of 1841 decreed that Br. Rice should sit for a portrait but it is in association with a related decree of the same Chapter that we are informed that "a portrait of the Founder was painted in Waterford by Robert Kennedy in the later months of 1841". No source is cited for that assertion nor is it clearly stated, nor even implied, that it was the wish of the Chapter. See *A Tree*, p. 374. We are informed in the *Biographical Register* of 1845 that McDowall's engraving was made from Kennedy's painting but Br. W. A. O'Hanlon, would only concede that McDowall based his engraving presumably on the Mount Sion portrait. The same man – most detailed of scholars! – was shrewd enough not to accept without question the attribution of either the Carrick or the Dungarvan portraits to Kennedy. He said they were "possibly by Kennedy". We now know the Carrick one is not by him and the Dungarvan one still awaits a restoration and examination. For O'Hanlon, see *The Educational Record* 1968. opposite p. 64.

5 *A Tree*, p. 374, taken from the House Annals of North Richmond St.

6 Br. O'Hanlon was careful to note that the portrait used for engraving was "presumably the Mount Sion one." *Educational Record* 1968, opposite p. 64.

7 Br. J. A. Grace had come as Superior to Nth Richmond St. in 1841.

8 Note again O'Hanlon's limited faith in this general belief. He conceded only that the Dungarvan and Carrick portraits were painted "possibly by Kennedy." See n. 6.

9 A view expressed by Mr. Le Harivel, Assistant Curator, National Galleries.

10 The majority of these subsequent likenesses were the creation of Samuel Watson and Mr. Le Harivel agreed that they were undoubtedly based on the Carrick portrait.

11 We had heard no reference to this until Mr. Hulme-Beaman had brought it to our attention. Since then I have heard, without asking, two variants of the basic story: one from Carrick-on-Suir and one from Waterford (Waterpark). Soap, improperly used, was central to both.

12 A new frame has been carefully chosen for the Carrick portrait.

13 He showed us two very similar slips which he had collected from other portraits.

14 Mr. Adrian Le Harivel has assured us that every effort will be made to have this date properly deciphered.

15 This question is much too large to be dealt with here. Moreover much further restoration and study of restored canvases will be necessary before answers can be suggested to these and similar other questions.

16 The only Robert Ken(n)edy of Waterford who might suit our dates was born on 7 December, 1809, to William Kenedy and Joanna (née Sulivan) and baptised in Ballybricken Parish Church, having as sponsors James Rice and Mary Quin. The priest was entered as 'J. P.' Information from the Waterford Heritage Centre – *quibus gratias agamus!*

17 From the house annals of Carrick-on-Suir, October (19)48.

18 Br. J. D. Goulding, who overheard this remark, died in September, 1959. He had repeated it for Br. E. B. Doyle before his death and the latter recorded the incident in 1964.

The Death of Brother Edmund Ignatius Rice in the Words of an Eyewitness

M. Austin Connolly, CFC

O UR EYEWITNESS is Br. Thomas Joseph Hearn. He was born in 1797 at Glin (now Glen) about five miles west of Carrick-on-Suir, on the road to Clonmel that runs along the south side of the river Suir. The river, at this point, is the boundary between the counties of Tipperary and Waterford, and between the parishes of Carrick-on-Suir and Carrickbeg. The Hearn farm, set in full view of famed Slievenamon lay in the parish of Carrickbeg. At Ballindesert, about three miles nearer to Carrick, the redoubtable Br. John Patrick Corbett (1784-1867) was born. Both men were closely connected with our Carrick house: Br. Hearn was Superior there in the years 1835-37, and 1838-41; Br. Corbett spent all his long religious life there, being Superior in the years 1817-35 and 1842-52. And both men were associated with the care of the Founder's daughter, Mary, who spent the last years of her life in Carrick, receiving from Br. Corbett the money given for her maintenance by Br. Hearn from Institute funds. They also supply the only testimony we have of the death of Mary Rice. In an account book, kept by Br. Hearn, is the notice:

> M. Rice. who from time to time received something for her maintenance (see July 6th 1858, opposite page) died in Carrick-on-Suir on the 23rd of January 1859, and was interred in the Church yard in Carrickbeg, January 24th '59.
>
> John P. Corbett

The notice is set in a ruled "box", no doubt to give it importance, and is initialled "TJH". This seems to suggest that Br. Hearn received the information from Br. Corbett. (Mary would have been seventy years old when she died.) In looking after the daughter, they were performing a last act of filial piety to the Founder.

The location of that "Church yard" is still a problem, not to mention the location of the grave. In Carrickbeg there were three graveyards, each within about fifty yards of the others: that of the Franciscan Friary, that of the Parish Church of St. Molleran and the older medieval one called Relig na Muc. It seems strange to us today that our two good Brothers thought it sufficient to mention "the Church yard in Carrickbeg", without specifying which of the three it was. Being natives of the parish and having lived for many years in the town, they were well aware of the existence of the three burial grounds, and we must conclude that to them, at least, it was clear which of the three was meant. It is interesting to note that on the flat-topped tombstone of the Hearn family in the Friary graveyard are carved the names, among others, of Br. Hearn's mother (Catherine Mullowney), of his brother Nicholas and of the latter's wife (Catherine Hurley). It is tantalising that Br. Hearn, so well acquainted with the graveyards in Carrickbeg, did not think it necessary to be more specific in indicating the burial place of Mary Rice.

Br. Hearn had close personal acquaintance with the Founder having lived in the same house with him for several years. He entered Mount Sion in February 1826 and did his Postulancy and Noviceship there during the next twelve months. In those days General Council, Community and Novices all dined at the same table. Later, in 1841, when Br. Hearn was elected Assistant to Br. Paul Riordan, he returned to Mount Sion and lived with Br. Rice for the last three years of the Founder's life. These years of living together provided the observant Br. Hearn with ample opportunity for studying and admiring the person and character of Edmund Ignatius Rice.

There were, however, other experiences of a different nature, which influenced his judgement of the Founder. We can begin to examine this more critical attitude by considering the phrase written many years later by Br. Francis Thornton. In a letter, dated 14 March 1861, to Br. M. Ignatius Kelly, Br. Thornton writes: "I have on this day received a letter from Br. Austin Grace which too clearly proves that the old Cork spirit of party still exists in full vigour".

Brs. Thornton, Kelly and Grace would represent those "fidelissimi" to Br. Rice. "The old Cork spirit of party" centred round the two Brothers Leonard and Br. M. P. Riordan, "trio in uno" as they described themselves. This "click" (sic), as Br. Thornton described them, included Br. Hearn.

In the Cork house there seems to have been criticism of the Founder. The "trio", younger men and more independent, accustomed to having to defend their enterprise when misunderstandings arose with Bishop Murphy of Cork, gradually assumed a critical, even hostile attitude to the ageing Founder. Perhaps they considered themselves better educated. There were certainly several brilliant men in the Cork community. Their reluctance to accept the Brief in 1822 did not altogether arise from the attitude of Bishop Murphy, who was less than willing to have them pass from his immediate control by accepting Edmund Rice as their Superior General. Indeed the Founder, on his part, had misgivings about accepting them and "admitted them under great doubt, his two Assistants being firmly opposed to their admission because of their noted eccentricities and imperiousness" (Br. B. Dunphy to Archbishop Murray of Dublin, 26 November 1840).

The "trio" eventually decided to accept the Brief. They came separately to Mount Sion in 1826. The two Leonards made their profession in the hands of the Founder and then returned to Cork; Br. Riordan, having accepted the Brief, returned to Cork to begin his Novitiate. In that year, 1826, Thomas Joseph Hearn, aged 29, was in Mount Sion as Postulant and Novice and made his first acquaintance with the "trio" from Cork.

The calling of the General Chapter, more correctly called General Assembly, in 1829, and the ensuing difficulties that the Founder had to endure thereat clearly show the opposition emanating from certain Brothers in Cork and indicate what Br. Thornton had in mind when he refers to the "Cork spirit of party".

Br. Hearn came to be absorbed into this circle. After his year of training in Mount Sion (where he had lived with the "trio"), and five months in Limerick, he was sent to Cork by the Founder in June 1827. There he taught with Br. M. P. Riordan in Sullivan's Quay school. Except for a brief period in Manchester, he remained in Cork until 1835, so that he had ample time to come under the influence of the "Cork spirit". At any rate, he enjoyed the confidence of Br. Riordan who was elected to succeed Br. Rice as Superior General in 1838. Br. Hearn was elected Assistant at the Chapter of 1841, and came to reside in Mount Sion, which once again became the seat of the Generalate. He was appointed by Br. Riordan Novice Master and principal of the school. Indeed, much of the management of the Institute was gradually entrusted to him, and he became, albeit unofficially, our first Bursar General, Secretary General and Archivist, as can be seen from the many large Registers which he compiled during his long years in office. (The numbering system he used in listing the Brothers is still current in the Irish Provinces of the Congregation.) He retained these functions until the General Chapter of 1880 when he retired from office. He died in 1882.

From 1841, then, he lived once again with the Founder, now in his eighties, and witnessed his decline and death. He has left us two written accounts of the last moments of Edmund Ignatius Rice. The longer one clearly shows his admiration for the venerable man but also his disapproval of the Founder's accumulation of "debts" and of his involvement in law suits.

The shorter account (perhaps written soon after the event?) is written in the neat characteristic hand of Br. Hearn on a small sheet of paper and is reproduced here in its entirety:

> Br. Ignatius Rice, being nearly two years confined to his Room in a childish state, attended by a Nurse, during which time he was not considered a fit subject for the Holy Sacrament, for want of intellect, by Dr. D. O'Brien or Rev. J. Cooke, his last ordinary confessor. He shewed symptoms of his approaching end on the 22nd day of August 1844, received extreme unction the 25th, and the Thursday morning following about 4 o'clock, his agony commenced, continued till between 11 and 12 same day, at which hour he departed this life on the 29th day of August 1844 at Mt. Sion, Waterford, in the 82nd year of his age.
>
> Brs. Joseph Murphy, T. J. Hearn, Patrick Ellis & Lewis Hoare present. May he rest in peace. Amen.
>
> (Generalate Archives, folder n. 0042)

The longer account is found in the large volume labelled "AN OUTLINE OF THE INSTITUTE". This account, hereunder reproduced, is written on folios 20v to 28r. But almost half of the text of these folios is devoted to an account of the Chapter of 1838, to statistics of members and foundations, and to the transcription of the text of Edmund Rice's last will and testament with its two codicils, all of which do not concern us here and so have been omitted. The date of composition of this part of the register can, from internal evidence, be assigned to the years 1858-59, or fourteen years after the death of the Founder:

> 1838, July 24th, Br. Edmond (*sic*) Ignatius Rice being now in his 76th year found his manly frame and vigorous intellect giving way under the heavy pressure on his body and mind in the long discharge of the duties of his office, convoked a general Chapter at Mount Sion, Waterford. and tendered his resignation of his office of Superior General of the Society, alledging his age and infirmity as a sufficient cause to be relieved from its duties. His resignation was accepted.

(Matter not relevant to this article has been omitted)

Many were the obstacles which Br. Rice had to surmount in the formation of his Institute in its infancy, and various were the difficulties with which he had to contend in conducting its progress to the stage at which it arrived when he resigned his office of Superior General this year, 1838.

Being a man of comprehensive mind, with a powerful grasp of intellect combined with an extensive knowledge of the world, of men, and of business and long experience, together with an unbounded goodness of heart which inclined him to lend his effectual and powerful assistance to all, without distinction who required his aid and spare no sacrifice of himself to help them as far as he was able in their spiritual or temporal necessities.

With these distinguished qualities and good dispositions, with the best of intentions he not unfrequently (sic) rushed with facility into many difficulties, perhaps beyond the bounds of discretion to do good for others which entangled him in the meshes of the law all the days of his life, and furnished his representatives with an abundant supply of annoyance even after his death.

This observation is not made with a view to reflect unfavourably on the past, which under the then existing circumstances may not be considered blameable, but as a cautionary suggestion to the future members of a Religious Institute to depend on Providence and never to go to law, unless it is manifestly sinful to decline or omit it.

187

The exertions made by Br. E.I. Rice to establish and maintain the Institute, and supply its growing wants, involved him in a debt due to different parties at the time of his resignation of office amounting to over £5,000.

This debt was chiefly created by borrowing money from different persons and charities to purchase interests and to build North Richmond Street.

Some of the interests purchased were in terminable leases, and with the liquidation of the purchase money, some of the interests vanished, some of the terms expired, some were ejected before their time as by change of circumstances they became of no value, leaving nothing to him or to his Representatives but the trouble of managing these concerns during the time of their continuance.

No small portion of this debt was caused by law expenses, freely rushing into suits to protect the poor, the friendless, the orphan or the widow, or to secure the rights of poorhouses, asylums or whatever may have been left for Charitable purposes or pious uses.

These proceedings kept his representatives engaged with difficulties for twenty years* after his resignation before they could satisfy the claims of his numerous creditors with the resources that came into his hands.

The limited pecuniary resources was not the only difficulty Mr. Rice had to contend with in establishing the Institute or extending the sphere of its usefulness during the term of his office: this object could not be effected without suitable and sufficient subjects – with a sufficient number of them – where were such to be found?

(Statistics of members and foundations omitted; also Edmund Rice's last will with its two codicils)

When Br. E. I. Rice had settled his temporal affairs in this way, Br. Edmond Austin Dunphy entered practically into the management of them. The useful and active life of Mr. Rice was at an end, his infirmities increased and day after day, his health sensibly declined, the two last years of his existence he became childish and unable to attend to his own personal

---

* Hence the text was written about 1858.

wants, hence it was necessary to have an attendant always with (him). The mind once so vigorous being over worked now became imbecile and all energy departed from his once powerful frame. So that during the last year of his life it could be said that he existed. During this time, he was confined to his room, under the care of an attendant with medical aid as often as found necessary.

On the 22nd of August (Thursday) 1844 he showed some symptoms of his approaching dissolution.

On the 25th (Sunday) he received Extreme Unction and on Thursday morning following about 4 o'clock his last agony commenced with heavy breathing, which became every moment more oppressive and increased in a few hours to a distressing rattle in the throat and a heaving of the chest but without any contortion or convulsive movement. Respiration became extremely difficult and between eleven and twelve o'clock that same day, being the 29th of August 1844, with a deep sigh he breathed his last. The writer was present during the time and witnessed his expiring breath.

On Saturday the 31st, the Rt. Rev. N. Foran, Bishop of the Diocese and 29 clergymen attended his funeral obsequies at Mount Sion and his remains were interred in the N.E. angle of the Cemetery adjoining the Establishment which on this occasion was *consecrated* by the Bishop as a Cemetery, the place being previously (only?) blessed. A plain rude stone cross marks the spot where the remains of this great man rest, with only a very simple epitaph, or rather a plain inscription viz.

Br. Edmond (sic) Ignatius Rice died August 29th 1844.
Founder of the Christian Schools in Ireland and England.
Aged 82 years. R.I.P.

The Rt. Rev. Dr. Foran. Bishop of Waterford, who had the highest esteem for Mr. Rice, and was personally attached to him, both having for many years exerted themselves conjointly and continued with many difficulties for the interests of religion in that diocese proposed to have his month's memory celebrated in the Waterford Cathedral, which was accordingly done on October 1st 1844.

His Lordship presided and was attended with over 40 Clergymen, some of them from the neighbouring diocese; all of whom his Lordship entertained at dinner that evening with hospitality worthy of that good-hearted prelate and sincere friend of the Institute and would allow none but himself to defray any portion of the expenses of that day.

Next his Lordship, with Thomas Francis Meagher, Esq., M.P., then Mayor of the city, convened a meeting which was respectably attended, "to take into consideration the propriety of erecting a respectable monument to perpetuate the name of Mr. Rice as a testimony of his valuable services to Society in founding the Christian Schools".

Resolutions to that effect being proposed and adopted by acclamation contributions poured in abundantly so that the Bishop with the leading citizens determined on erecting something more useful than a marble slab.

They decided on building an additional school at Mount Sion, with a domestic chapel for the community as the most appropriate testimony to the zeal of the deceased. This was carried into effect at an expense of £900.

The following inscription placed inside, over the entrance to the domestic chapel, specifies the object of its erection:

'As a tribute of
Gratitude for the Services and Respect for the Virtues
of
Brother Edmund Ignatius Rice
Founder of the Christian Schools in Ireland and England
His friends and Admirers of both Countries
Have Erected this
Edifice
Sacred to the objects
which,
During his long and valuable career
were the dearest to his Heart.
He departed this life on the 29th August 1844, Aged 82 years.
Requiescat in Pace.'

This great man and benefactor of the human race, destined from all eternity to fulfil his mission, and to be "The Founder of the Society of the Religious Brothers of the Christian Schools in Ireland", was born of respectable parents at West Court, in the immediate vicinity of Callan in the Co. Kilkenny, in the month of June 1762.

He received an elementary education in Callan and completed his course in Kilkenny.

At the age of seventeen years, he went to live with his uncle Michael Rice, who chiefly followed the provision trade, and was then a wealthy merchant in the City of Waterford. After a few years, he succeeded his uncle in that business and was very successful, and by his surpassing talents for business, was already accumulating a fortune leading to rank, influence and independence.

In the fortieth year of his age and in the prime of life, he conceived serious thoughts of changing his course and retire into solitude away from the busy scenes of the world, to spend his days in religious retirement and secure his salvation.

Providence ordained otherwise, and while divided between the active and contemplative life, which to choose, he recommended the matter earnestly to God: he prayed; he took advice, and having once decided, his vocation was fixed.

He was a man of tall stature, six feet, not corpulent, but with large and full limbs, well proportioned and shaped. His mien and carriage were dignified and graceful, his features marked but agreeable, his forehead high, his brows heavy and arched, which he could contract or expand with ease so as to give an expression to his countenance that manifestly indicated how he thought and felt at the moment. His glance was pleasing and piercing at the same time. The eye brilliant, with the sight keen and good, so as to read without glasses to the end. His voice and tone were manly but soft and agreeable, without any tincture of effeminacy. His manners, from his great intercourse with people of all classes, were considerably refined and pleasing, and his conversation cheerful and grave at the same time.

He possessed in an eminent degree those qualities to be found only in great souls: a remarkably powerful and vigorous intellect, a comprehensive knowledge of human nature, a consummate prudence, an unbending courage, indomitable energy and untiring perseverance, which sustained (him?) under the many trying difficulties he had to contend with during the 40 years since he first conceived the idea of embracing a religious life till he resigned his office of Superior General of the Institute he formed and founded and conducted to 1838.

Br. Edmond Ignatius Rice won the affection of all the Brethren; he lived beloved, he died lamented. "He fought the good fight, he kept the faith". His memory is in benediction, May his soul rest in peace."

(Generalate Archives, folder n. 0035)

The above account of the Founder's youth seems to rely on the MS. "An Account of the Origin, Rise and Progress of the Institute of the Society of Religious Brothers", sometimes referred to as "Origin", written by Br. E. A. Dunphy. (cf. Br. W. A. O'Hanlon in *Educational Record* 1979 pp. 16 & 20.)

If someone should remark on the style of Brother Hearn's English, he should remember that the Brother, like many of his contemporaries from the rural parts of South and West Ireland, including the Founder, grew up in homes where Irish (Gaelic) was the spoken language. An unnamed contemporary has this to say of Br. Hearn: "Besides his knowledge of Mathematics and English, he spoke and read Irish fluently, and was well read in the French and Latin languages".   (*Educational Record* 1895 p.229)